THE ART OF PAINTING

Under the Great Mughals

THE ART *of* PAINTING

Under the Great Mughals

(A.D. 1526 to 1707 A.D.)

T. N. Mishra

AGAM KALA PRAKASHAN

DELHI

First Published 2014

ISBN : 978 -81-7320-140-0

Published by:
Dr. Agam Prasad, M.A., Ph.D., Diploma in Museology
For **Agam Kala Prakashan**
34, Central Market, Ashok Vihar
Delhi - 110 052
Tel.: 27212195, 65688806-7
Fax: 91-11-27212195
Email: agambooks@gmail.com, agambook@yahoo.com
www.agamkala.com

Composed by:
Aman Printographics
Delhi - 110 052
Mobile: 9891395309

Printed by:
Chawla Offset Printers
Wazirpur Village, Ashok Vihar
Delhi-110 052

Printed in India

Contents

Preface 7

Acknowledgements 9

List of Illustrations 11

Introduction 17

The Great Mughal Rulers and their Reign-periods 27

Names of Painters of the Great Mughals 77

Bibliography 87

Index 91

Description of Plates 101

Preface

The titanic and complex personality of the great Mughal is not easy to portray. We have contemporary portraits of the emperor – one from the pen of the writers or historians and other from the brush of his court artists.

The Mughal emperors were keen lovers of nature and art. And their personality was reflected in the art and culture of their times. The Mughal dynasty in the India was founded by Babur in 1526 A.D. Babur's Indian sojourn of four years until his untimely death in 1530 A.D. appears to be too brief to leave any lasting legacy. The state of uncertainty in the days of Babur and Humayun was not, however, favourable, for any outstanding contribution to the development of art and culture. But the beginning of a new brush-work was started under Humayun when he was in exile.

Indeed Akbar took an important part in the evolution of the Mughal art by the happy fusion and harmonious blending of Persian and Indian art. He himself was the symbol of that synthesis. He gave a new orientation to the Indo-Islamic art. Thus the art of painting was founded with novel trends.

Under the aesthetic Jahangir, with his intelligent patronage, the art of painting reached it meridian. His sophistication was also marked with the use of marble in architecture. The glory of the art of painting was maintained in a slightly less degree during magnificent reign of Shah Jahan. Shah Jahan's name is, however, chiefly associated with the art of architecture, because many noble buildings were erected in his reign for which he is most widely renowned.

The decline of the arts began with Aurangzeb, who gave little encouragement to his people in the sphere of artistic expressions. With the death of the Emperor Aurangzeb, the story of Mughal painting begins to draw to a close.

Acknowledgements

In the collection of related materials for this volume the author is indebted to many scholars and institutions of India and abroad. Of these, mention may be made of those scholars who have been consulted during the preparation of this volume; their contribution are mentioned in the bibliography.

I am grateful for help and suggestions of Prof. Dr. Deena Banadhu Pandey, formerly Head, Department of History of Art, Banaras Hindu University.

My thanks are also due to Bharat Kala Bhavan, B.H.U., Varanasi, National Museum, New Delhi, Indian Museum, Calcutta, Prince of Wales Museum, Bombay, Sawai Man Singh II Museum, Jaipur.

I am thankful to my wife Vandana and my daughters Kavita, Pratima and Jyoti, who gave me encouragement in preparation of the manuscript.

T.N. Mishra

List of Illustrations

Pl.1. The White Elephant
Early 17th Century A.D.
Bharat Kala Bhavan, Varanasi

Pl. 2. Bull Fighting
C. 1605 A.D.
Artist – Farrukh
Private Collection

Pl. 3. Elephant Hawaii
C. 1590 A.D.
Artist – Composed by Basawan and painted by Chitra

Pl. 4. A Lion Court
Mughal
Artist – Farrukh Chela
Bharat Kala Bhavan, Varanasi

Pl. 5. Lion Court (The Assembly of Animals)
C. 1596 A.D.
Artist – Miskin
Bharat Kala Bhavan, Varanasi

Pl. 6. A Carcass of a Dead Camel Mughal
Artist – Miskin
Bharat Kala Bhavan, Varanasi

Pl. 7. Killing of helpless bull
C. 1592 A.D.
Artist – Nand Gwaliori
Bharat Kala Bhavan, Varanasi

Pl. 8. Camel rider rescuing the Snake Mughal
Bharat Kala Bhavan, Varanasi

Pl. 9. A Ram
C. 1558 A.D.
Artist – Basawan
Maharaja Sawai Mansingh II Museum, Jaipur

Pl. 10. A Story of Old Ass
Artist – Lalchhaman
Bharat Kala Bhavan, Varanasi

Pl. 11. Elephant
C. 1590 A.D.
Artist – Basawan

Pl. 12. Misconception of Approaching Death Mughal
Artist – Mukund
Bharat Kala Bhavan
Varanasi

Pl. 13. The Farmer Retrieves his Money Miraculously
Mughal
Artist – Bishandas
Bharat Kala Bhavan, Varanasi

Pl. 14. Mesh Rashi (Aris)
Late 16th Cent. A.D. (C. 1570 A.D.)
Bharat Kala Bhavan, Varanasi

Pl. 15. Jahangir shows his hunting skill
C. 1615 A.D.
Artist – Manohar
Indian Museum
Calcutta

Pl. 16. Emperor on hunt
C. 1598 – 1600 A.D.
National Museum, New Delhi

Pl. 17. Horse
Mughal School (Akbari period)

Pl. 18. Squirrels in a tree
C. 1615 A.D.
Artist – Abu-l-Hasan

Pl. 19. Falcon
C. 1619 A.D.
Artist – Mansur
Maharaja Sawai Mansingh II Museum, Jaipur

Pl. 20. Falcon (Baaz)
Mid 17th Century
Artist – Mansur

Pl. 21. Himalyan Cheer Pheasent
Circa 1640 A.D.
Artist – Mansur
Maharaja Sawai Mansingh II Museum, Jaipur

Pl. 22. Zebra
C. 1612 / 1621 A.D.
Artist – Mansur

Pl. 23. Turkey cock
C. 1612 A.D.
Artist – Mansur
Maharaja Sawai Mansingh II Museum
Jaipur

Pl. 24. Hen and Chicks
Mughal School
C. 1605-27 A.D.
Artist – Ustad Mansur

Pl. 25. Maina
C. 1625-30 A.D.
Probably – Mansur
Prince of Wales Museum, Bombay

Pl. 26. Jungle Fowl
C. 1611 A.D.
Artist – Mansur

Pl. 27. Emperor holding the hawk
C. 1600 A.D.
Jahangiri Period

Pl. 28. Ensnared Deer
Folio from an illustrated Ms of Anwar-i-Suhali
C. 1575 - 1680 A.D.
Prince of Wales Museum
Bombay

Pl. 29. Himalayan Ibex (Mountain goat)
Early 17th Cent. A.D.
Prince of Wales Museum, Bombay

Pl. 30. Lion drinking water
C. 1618 A.D.
Artist – Nanha
Maharaja Sawai Mansingh II Museum, Jaipur

Pl. 31. Dara Shikoh with Sages
Artist – Bichitra

Pl. 32. Darbar of Alamgir (Aurengzeb)
Artist – Bichitra
Private Collection

Pl. 33A & B. Aurengzeb Hunting Nilgai
C. 17th Century
Artist – Bichitra
Bharat Kala Bhavan, Varanasi

Introduction

India is a country rich in history and cultural heritage. From the Indus Valley Civilization to the Mughal empire, different cultures have written different stories for themselves across the subcontinent. These civilizations accumulated and left behind the artifacts of their times, as their communities expended and evolved.

Interpreting the way of life, behaviour and habits of the people who lived in the past, through the material things they left behind is the primary job of an art-historian. Moreover, art-historian is expected always to be completely objective in his work so as to present an honest interpretation of the finds.

Artifacts relating to our country are historical revelations. Those portraying vivid aspects of India, the varied costumes and customs of its people, have a special fascination for people today. Pictorially, the range of subjects is vast. It includes historical episodes, military events, customs, costume, social life, natural history, fields of sports and portraiture as well as occupations of the Indian people.

The character of the art of a country is very often determined by its physical conditions. The human mind cannot ignore external surroundings; and art is an expression of human thought and feeling. It invariably relates consciously or unconsciously, to the physical conditions under which it finds expression. Thus we find that the variations and changes in the art of a country corresponds to the vicissitudes through which it has to pass, and art is no exception. Indian art has a long history and shows a variety of artistic expressions of different periods. They help to understand the mental state of the Indian people under different conditions, their character and emotions; all of which contribute towards the varied artistic forms of the country.

The contemporary pattern of Indian culture is a confluence of various cultural streams that have been flowing into India ever since the dawn of her history. The Indian cultural pattern has expanded and grown richer with the passage of time, this was due to its adaptive characteristics which made assimilation and accommodation of obtruding cultures possible.

The art was one of the media through which the people of India sought to interpret this oneness of life. The artist displayed a sense of loving awareness of the various forms of life that surrounded him and unfolded the moving process of life itself by tying up regulation, animal and bird life in the web of human existence.

The artistic heritage of India may be roughly said to have been handed down to posterity from about 3000 B.C. Ever since, this tradition has continued with hardly any break, till today. Though Indian art has shaped, re-shaped and been moulded time and again under the influence of various socio-cultural and political factors, yet ultimate aim remains unchanged. Art's ultimate aim has always been deliverance from the snare of illusion and attainment of the great delight through the experience of truth and ultimate beauty. Art in its varied facets has been depicted through different media. Innumerable evidences of historical importance have been discovered through archaeological excavations and explorations of various monuments and sites in India, alongwith a large amount of literary reference too.

Art reflects contemporary society. The art of the period possesses tremendous potentialities in reconstructing the history of the period. This holds good also with reference to paintings like other source materials, Indian painting played a very significant role in this endeavour. Although unrelentless efforts are still being made to discover evidences of pre-historic rock paintings in the hilly tracts of Utttar Pradesh and Madhya Pradesh. Tangible evidences of rock paintings dating back to the first or second century B.C. can be seen in the rock cave paintings at Ajanta. Thereafter, the tradition of Indian paintings maintained an unbroken continuity. Other exemplary evidences of paintings have been noticed in Buddhist rock-cut caves in mountains of Western Ghats namely, Ajanta, Bedsa, Kanhari and Pitalkhora. Cave painting have also been noticed at Sittannavasal, Kanchipuram, Tirumalaipuram, etc. The codification of painting in text began in the Gupta period. Thereafter till the twentieth century continued the exemplification of the various aspects of painting. These include canonical texts, historical accounts and traveller's reports.

The first phase of Indian painting called the classical phase reached its logical acme in the Gupta-Vakataka period. Though evidences of classical paintings were seen in the Buddhism related Pala manuscripts, in eastern India, a new trend in Indian painting developed at around the 8th century A.D. which first noticed at Ellora, and was termed as the 'medieval phase'. Patronage from religious establishments went a long way in promoting arts of both the 'classical' as well as 'medieval phases' as is evident in the miniature paintings and manuscripts of the Pala period and also the Jain paintings, which are seen at the Buddhist Mahaviharas and Jaina Bhandaras.

During the first period of post-classical art in India, i.e. from the thirteenth to sixteenth century A.D., Muslim ruler achieved almost complete political control. The advent of Islam constituted the first great rift in the Indian community, resulting in decline in artistic patronage given by the Hindu ruler. The artistic interests of the Muslim rulers was layed primarily in architecture. The art of painting was condemned by Muslim rulers as a blasphemous imitation of God's creativity. The traditions of painting suffered as a result of this neglect. The Hindu Sisodiya of Mewar is a notable exception. During the fifteenth century A.D., the Sisodiya ruler, built numerous forts and temples which were decorated with beautiful wall paintings.

It appears that the art of miniature painting did not get any patronage from the Sultans of Delhi. Though many of them built up large libraries, which may have contained illustrated manuscripts with decorative patterns, not a single miniature has so for been definitely identified belonging to the court of Delhi Sultan. But the provincial Sultans could not keep themselves aloof from art activities. The situation was different in provinces, where manuscripts were prepared and illustrated with paintings. Though the heritage of classicism is undeniably rich and unforgettable, yet a new culture and civilization with different outlook, i.e. the Mughal era changed the direction and transformed the India's life and thought. In painting the classism did not show a strong creative urge and surrendered its place to a new medieval style called Mughal art.

Now we can see, the medieval period witnessed another important change where art was concerned, due to infiltration and invasion of India by the Zahir-ud-din Muhammed Babur, the founder of the Mughal dynasty. A unique blend between medieval traits and the new Persian styles and techniques developed under the Mughals, which absorbed and assimilated a number of trends, viz. Sultanate mannerism, trends from Kashmir and other hilly areas, western idioms from Europe and certain Central Asian mannerisms too, and in due course of time resulted the electrical Mughal paintings.

It must be admitted that Babar's influence on the artistic development of India was immense, although this did not show itself during his lifetime. The Mughal emperors were keen lovers of nature and art and their personality was, to a certain extent, reflected in the art and culture of their time. From the sixteenth century onward, Mughal and Hindu rulers reinvigorated the tradition of painting ensconced in their Tumurid heritage and culture, greatly appreciated painting. The Mughal school of painting represents one of the most significant phase of Indian art. Mughal miniatures show some thing never before seen in India, and their lasting effect reverberated throughout India after the Mughal vanished. For the proper understanding of the Mughal painting, its scene, themes and history, one must study of the memoirs of the Mughal emperors, Babar, Humayun, Akbar and Jahangir. They are primary source of information on painters and paintings of Mughal school. The dynasty as it was so keenly interested in the arts that each emperor, as he came into power, put something of himself into the painting of his reign. To follow the development of Mughal painting, therefore, it is necessary to understand something of the individual temperament of those monarchs who did so much for its encouragement.

The Babar-Nama is also an illustrated social and natural history of India. The figures are shown in movement, and their highly expressive gestures convey their feelings.

The Babur was the first natural history scientist who made accurate and incisive observation on the fauna and flora of India. Babur was the founder of the Mughal dynasty in India. But could not get time to stable the Mughal power. He was a man of indomitable will, a great soldier and an inspiring leader. But unlike most men of action he was also a man of letters with fine literary taste and fastidious critical perception.

The state of uncertainty in days of Humayun was not, however, favourable, for any outstanding contribution to the development of art and culture. The beginnings of Mughal painting was laid by Humayun during the year of his exile in Persia and Afghanistan.

Indeed Akbar took an important part in the evolution of Mughal culture by the happy fusion and harmonious blending of Persion and Indian cultures; he himself was the very symbol of that synthesis. He was a man of original ideas and bold conceptions. He gave a new orientation to Indo-Islamic history. The Akbar-Nama was written by Abul Fazal, a courtier of Akbar. It is a scholarly work and contains details about history, administration as well as the arts and crafts of India in the sixteenth century. In fact, it is the first gazetteer of India. The Tuzk Jahangir records the wild animals, birds and garden plants of India, and contains a sensitive accounts of gardens of Kashmir. It revails Jahangir's love for nature. Shah Jahan was not seriously interested in painting as his interest lay on architecture and decorative arts. He embellished old structure with the purity of white marble, built new forts and masques. He clothed the robustness of Akbari creation beauty and poetic grace with the help of decoration. The Tasavir Khana (Surat Khana), however, continued to thrive as a necessary adjunct of the imperial establishment. There were few paintings and very small number of illustrated manuscripts produced by Mughal Surat Khana (art-studio), but in their naturalistic beauty, refinement and technical perfections they still maintained. This period was so rich and prolific in the field of arts, that many beautiful masterpieces were painted.

The most important product of his reign is the Padashah Nama manuscript like his grandfather Akbar, he intrusted his court historians to record the official account of his reign. Shah Jahan was interested in portraiture and several albums containing formal portrait studies himself, of his sons, Mullahs and Dervish, and leading courtiers have come down to us. Experienced painters painted many wonderful portraits. In the course of his long rule. Shah Jahan largely transformed the form and content of Mughal painting and took away much of its creativeness and élan and only occasional sparks are discernible in the limited production of the imperial creation. The painting of Shah Jahan lack the personal touch of an art loving patron like his father Jahangir. Owing to illness and age, the hand of the Emperor Shah Jahan began to relinquish its hold on the affairs of the empire, the art, too, had reached its first stage of dissolution.

Shah Jahan's eldest son Dara Shikoh took keen interest in painting. This gifted prince was a collector of these works of art, as is proved by a precious album of miniatures bearing his signature and now in the India office library, London.

Shah Jahan's third son Aurangzeb deposed his father in the year 1658 A.D. From Akbar to Aurangzeb (A.D. 1556 to 1657 A.D.), a little more than hundred year, cover the whole period during which the Mughal school of painting was a living art. From now begins the story of its decay. To Aurangzeb's unsympathetic policy the decline of the Mughal has been ascribed, and to his puritanical personality the death of the painter's art is attributed. Among institutions which collapsed was the Mughal school of painting.

The beginning of the Mughal Empire and the eventual demise can be traced back to the reign of Aurangzeb in the late seventeenth century. Taking a broad view of the state of things at the death of Aurangzeb, it is difficult to ignore the fact that inspite of the brilliant qualities of head and heart which enabled the emperor to extend the Mughal Empire over the whole of Deccan and South India, the grave defects of his character are mainly responsible for the sudden collapse of the mighty empire which then included nearly the whole of India and Afghanistan. Mughal empire reached the highest point only to break down, and Aurangzeb must share both credit and discredit for the same, at least to a very large extent. But it was not merely the fall of an empire but also the end of an epoch which ushered in a period of decline and distress after a century of peace and prosperity under the strong and wise governments of three generations before Aurangzeb. Peace and security "the sole justification of Mughal Empire" no longer existed in India at the time of Aurangzeb's death. The latter Mughal rulers had neither the ability nor the strength of character to pilot the ship of state properly and political unity which the great Mughals had managed to maintain in some form or the other for about two centuries disappeared under their effeminate successors exposing the country to various disintegrating forces.

With the death of Emperor Aurangzeb in 1707 A.D. the story of Mughal painting begins to draw to a close. The disintegration of the Mughal empire brought about the dispersal of the school of painting which belong to it; its death-kneel was rung when artists began to desert the Mughal capital on the decline of the court there.

The Great Mughal Rulers and their Reign-periods

The Great Mughal Rulers and their Reign-periods

1. **Zahir-ud-din Muhammad Babur**
   - A.D. 1526-1530 A.D.
2. **Nassir-ud-din Muhammad Humayun**
   - A.D. 1530-1556 A.D.
3. **Abu'l Fath Jalal-ud-din Muhammad Akbar**
   - A.D. 1556-1605 A.D.
4. **Nur-ud-din Muhammad Jahangir**
   - A.D.1605-1627 A.D.
5. **Shahab-ud-din Muhammad Sahib Qiran Sani Shah Jahan**
   - A.D. 1627-1658 A.D.
6. **Abu'l Zafar-ud-din Muhammad Aurengzeb Alamgir**
   - A.D. 1657-1707 A.D.

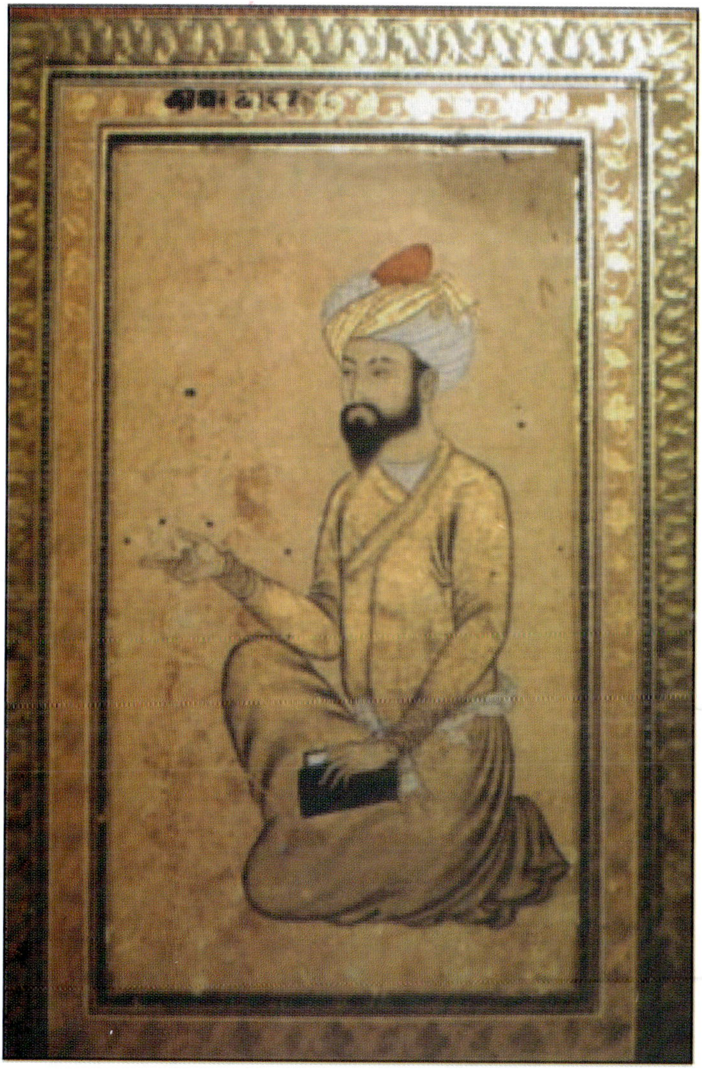

Zahir-ud-din Muhammad Babur
A.D. 1526-1530 A.D.

Babur the founder of the Mughal dynasty in India, is regarded as one of the most romantic and interesting personalities of Indian history. He was a man of indomitable will, a great soldier, and an inspiring leader. He was a man of action and man of letters with fine literary taste.

All of the Great Mughal emperors were interested in the art of painting that each one, as he came into power, put something of himself into the painting of his reign. To follow the development of Mughal painting, therefore, it is necessary to understand something of the individual temperament of those monarchs who did so much for its encouragement. Though Babur's influence on the artistic development was immense, but it could not revealed itself during his lifetime. It is therefore to say that Babur's ideals guided to art activity and inspired. But Babur had no love for this country. On the whole a somewhat unfavourable opinion about India, as on more than one occasion he expressed his feeling on the barrenness of the country and shortcomings of its people. Therefore, with such attitude for the country and for the people it was difficult to initiate any creative art movement.

Babur excelled in music and art, he was a learned philosopher, a mighty hunter, an enthusiastic traveler, an eager student of the habits and appearance of animals and birds, and specially devoted to flowers, gardens and beauties of nature. And above all he was a born artist- as shown on almost in every page of his own memoirs. Babur-Nama, Tuzuk-i-Baburi or Wakait-i-Baburi. His life was sent to battle filed, with little prospects of any prolonged period of leisure in which he might have given reign to his artistic inclinations.

Babur's Indian sojourn of four years from 1526 to 1530 until his death, appears to be too brief to leave any lasting legacy, but, infact, it was sufficient to change the entire course of Indian history as also to leave perceptible impact on its culture, society and political atmosphere. This was entirely due to his multifaceted personality, glimpse of which are found in his autobiography, the Babur Nama. He excelled and was proficient in music and art. The great lover of nature by no means less sensitive to the charms of fauna of India. He writes in detail and with enthusiasm about a number of animals and birds of India, and his observations are remarkable literary pieces of zoological statistics. He describes the immense size and sagacity of the elephant, and how it eats and drinks with its trunk and uses its tusks in fighting or in felling trees and knocking down walls. He gives interesting data to distinguish the different species of monkey and notices the affinity between the rhinoceros and horse, and between the squirrel and the mouse. He writes also about the wild buffalo, nilgai (blue-bull), the deer and many others. Among the birds he notices peacocks, floricans, monals, pheasants, herons, hoopoes, pigeons, ducks and pelicans and separates and describes five types of parrots. He was a born aesthete with a keen sense of perception for the beauties of nature and art. He was amazed by what he saw in India. Considering the age in which he lived he can rightly claim to be the first natural history scientist of India.[1]

The Mughal concern for naturalism - details which are colourful, meticulous and pulsating with life - apparent from the very beginning of Mughal painting definitely originates from Babur's deep concern for man and nature and his penchant for details. In fact, no one of his family before him ever possessed such talents as he.

---

1 M.S. Randhwa, *Roopa-Lakha*, Vol. XLII, No. I & II, p. 14.

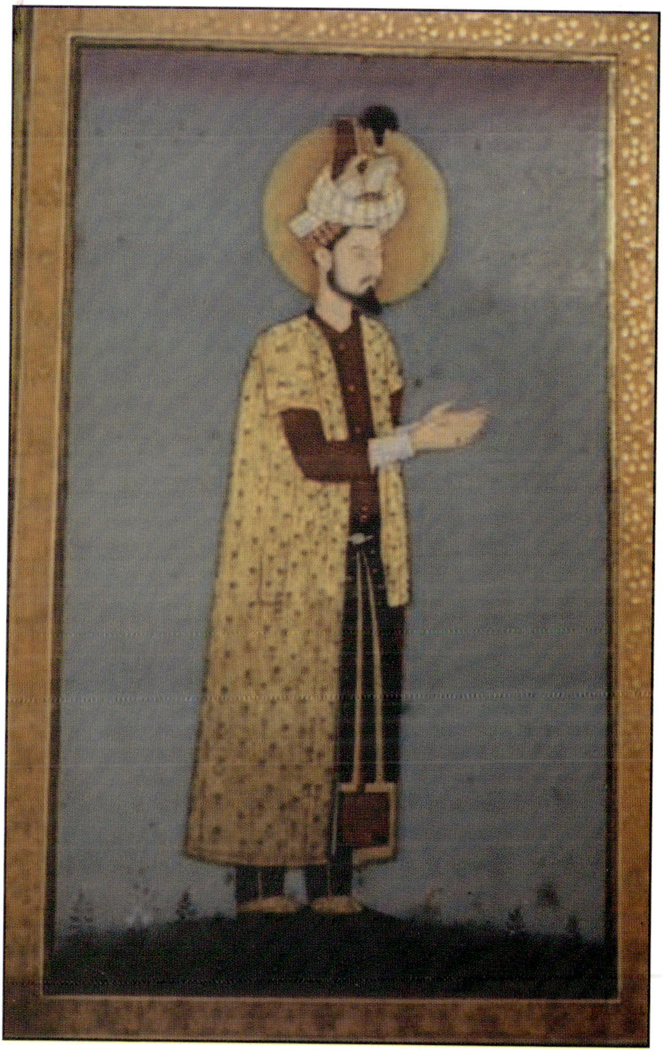

Nassir-ud-din Muhammad Humayun
A.D. 1530-1556 A.D.

Babur was succeeded by his son Humayun, who, while inheriting scholarly attributes of his father, was by no means in character or administrative ability. Humayun himself was a learned man as he was reared up in an atmosphere of sophisticated culture. From his childhood, Humayun received a good training in arts, literature and music, besides other subjects. He was also a fine calligrapher like his father.

Humayun was a man of ability, but was too weak a ruler to hold on effectively for long; consequently he lost the throne of Delhi in 1540 A.D. and driven out from India by Sher Shah, and take refuge in Iran, where Shah Tahmasp's hospitality, lacked with calculated slight, was the prelude to his guest's in himself or gave up the hope during this period from A.D. 1540-1555 A.D. He saw himself again the ruler of his lost empire. During the whole period of exile, Humayun found time for many peaceful occupations, in which he utilized the services of his artist from Tabriz. It is related that he took lesson in drawing and interested himself in the subjcct of painting.

The initial step in its beginning and development of school of painting was taken by the Emperor Humayun, by retaining the two artists from Persia in his services, while visiting Tabriz he met Abdus-Samad, a calligrapher and painter of considerable repute, and extended his invitation to him to join his court. When Humayun returned to Kabul and started his own court both Mir Sayyid Ali and Abd-us-Samad were given good positions. Both were appointed as painting instructors of his young son Akbar.

This achievement of Humayun lies in his momentous decision to have his own painting studio in spite of uncertain existence at Kabul and to recruit the services of two of finest Persian Masters already famous for their highly realistic and expressive style, thus paving the way for remarkable achievement of the Mughal school in next few decades.

All the successors of Babur, who together with him are known as the Great Mughals of Indian history had in fact each one of them showed his adoration for the name in the one form or the other. Humayun on ascending the throne ordered All'u-l-Katib to copy of his father's Turki book and see to it that the work was finished in less than a month and a half. Humayun's main interests lay in poetry and love for flowers and gardens too. He was fond of mobile gardens on boat which astonished and amazed every one.[1] It was, however, a short-lived glory of Humayun, for a few months later he died. And young Akbar was proclaimed emperor in 1556 A.D.

---

1 Gulbadan Begam, *Humayun-Nama*, Tree Annettee Beveridge, London, 1902, p. 126.

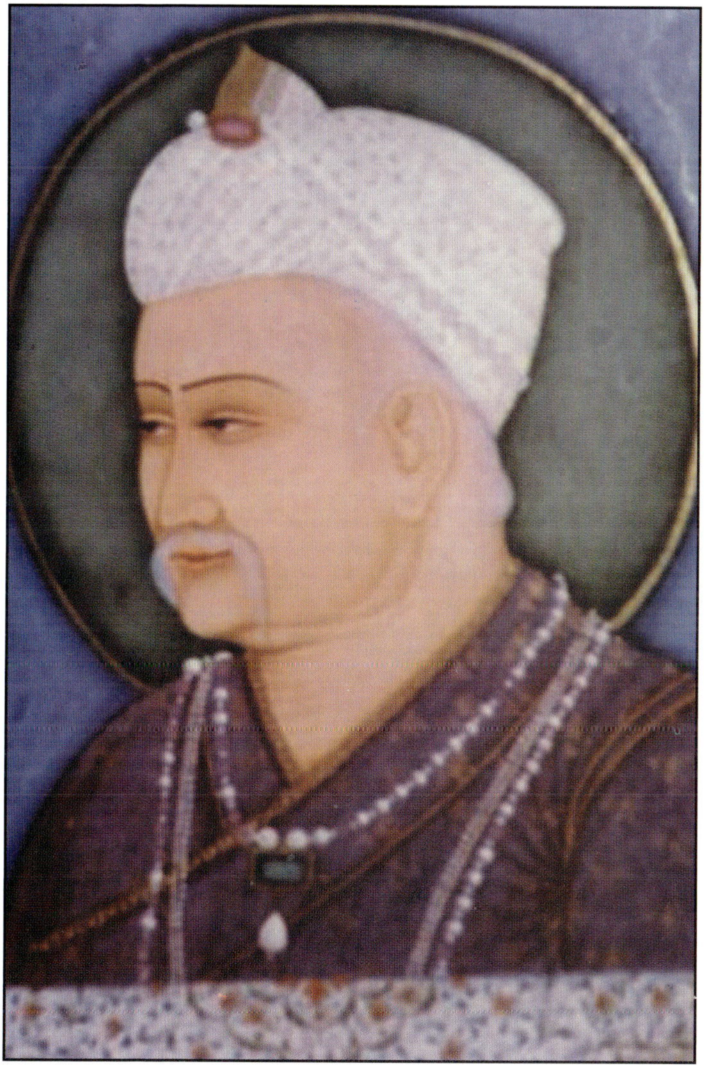

Abu'l Fath Jalal-ud-din Muhammad Akbar
A.D. 1556-1605 A.D.

Jalal-ud-din Muhammed Akbar was, one of the greatest of Indian monarchs, Akbar saw what both Babur and Humayun had never seen-the inherent capabilities of Indian people, their culture, their aspirations, and their ideals. He realized that the failure of his forebears and also of his co-religionists, who had established themselves in various parts of India, to maintain anything like harmonious rule was due in a measure to their lack of sympathy with the Hindustani races, to a disregard of their manners and customs, their arts and mental outlook.

Emperor Akbar was a ruler who had the vision of an unified Hindustani culture, and a man who had an abounding love for Hindustan. He therefore, consciously propounded an idealism which lead to the development of an art and culture based essentially to begin to be modulated by an Indian feeling. However, Akbar's reign, was a period of transition and reconstruction in art and culture. After a few years of uncertainty he quickly held the reins of his fast-growing empire in his firm grip with extraordinary courage, steadfastness and an uncanny political sagacity.

The greatness of Akbar lies in his originality of thought, in his wide comprehension and political insight and in his unceasing quest for knowledge. Akbar did not take formal education due to his unsettled childhood. The result was that in a family of learned and cultured princes he remained practically unlettered. He, of course, made up this serious shortcoming more than adequately by associating with learned men and holding intellectual discussions on religion, philosophy and related subjects at frequent intervals. There is not a single art, not a single branch of knowledge, not a single act of boldness and strength which was not attempted by emperor Akbar. The impact of his great personality thoroughly transformed the entire character of the age. Now Akbar find leisure to devote his abilities to the encouragement of learning, and began to task of arousing within his subjects an interest in the art of peace.

Akbar conceived the idea of reviving the pictorial art of India by means of properly organized school of painting and the first step was taken to put the art of painting on a suitable footing by creating a department for its development. He had been encouraged to do so by his father Humayun. Akbar and his father were both interested in painting. Miniature painting was therefore only one of many arts and industries which at this time were imparted into India to undergo a transformation in the hands of skilled craftsmen. The emperor Akbar, personally interested in its development, took definite measures for its encouragements, maintaining as a part of their retinue a staff of artists, skilled in this form of painting, and employing them in working out in their own ideas. So, in course of time the Mughal school of miniature painting, reflected in its subject matter and in its intention the mind of the ruling power.

The golden period of Akbar's school of painting was that in which the artists connected with it were working at Fatehpur Sikri, his new capital, the most important centre of creative activities of all kinds of art and craft. Emperor Akbar collected and provided patronage to architects, artists, craftsmen, poets, writers, painters, both from Hindu and Muslims who worked under the Persian Master artists-Abd-us-Samad and Mir Sayyid Ali, and result was that a new style of painting evolved, which is Indian in spirit and Persian in technique. Now the painting of this school are called Mughal painting.

Within a brief span of time he not only consolidated his position as an empire builder but also embarked upon his pursuits in art and architecture. In an atmosphere of such syncretistic ideas, art and culture are found to flourish. Akbar by virtue of his early training, took a keen interest in painting. A separate department known as Taswir Khana was created to cater for the needs of the large number of painters, calligraphers illuminators, gilders, margin-cutters, paper makers, polishers, book binders, colour grinders, gold beaters etc. working there. There was always a good rapport between the patron and his painters, the latter often confirming to the ideas of the former. To him a work of art had much more importance than its outward appearance. In the word of Abul Fazl, a picture was a 'source of wisdom, and an antidote against the poison of ignorance' for a well regulated mind. And here follows a sentence which points directly to the cause of their somewhat elaborate reflection, 'Bigoted followers of the letter of the law are hostile to the art of painting, but their eyes now see the truth.' Akbar's own remarks on the subject, 'there are many that hate painting, I cannot tolerate those who make the slightest criticism of the art, but such men I dislike. It appears to me as if a painter had quite peculiar means of recognising God; for a painter in sketching anything that has life, and devising its limbs, one after the other, must come to feel that he can not bestow individuality upon his work and is thus forced to think of God, the Giver of life and will, thus increase his knowledge.'

The unorthodox views of the emperor helped the painters to take calculated attempts to abandon the formality and rigid conventions of Muslim religious idioms. These sentiments speak for themselves, their objects being to show that Akbar's liking for pictures was so pronounce that he was prepared to put aside his religious convictions in order to enjoy to the full his pleasure in the art of painting.[1]

For the need of art Emperor Akbar looked deeply into the matter of raw materials required by the painters and set a high value on the quality of production. As a result, delicacy of works, clarity of lien and boldness of execution have reached perfection and colouring and finishing has gained new beauty. Such excellent artists have assembled to provide a wonderful works of the world. The court historian records how the emperor personally discovered the potential talent of Daswant and helped him to become 'the first master of the age, whose works were not behind those of Bihzad.

The masterpieces of painting increased with the encouragement given to the art and artist. Persian books (both prose and poetry) were ornamented with pictures and large number of painting was collected. The story of Hamza-Nama[2] has been illustrated and have painted astonishing pictures of may incidents. The Babar-Nama, Khandan-i-Timuriya, the Zafar-Nama, Akbur-Nama, Razm-Nama, Iyar-

1 The authority of these opinions is Abul Fazl in *A'in-i-Akbari-*

Akbar was very fond of the romantic fantasies in the mythical stories of Hamza. Hamza was the uncle of Prophet, and his adventures are narrated in the book named 'Hamzanama' after him. These are large size of painting on cloth, in Persian style. It seems that stimulus was provided by the illiteracy of Akbar. As he was unable to read, he felt the use of paintings as a visual aid.

Art was one of the media through which the people of India sought to interpret this oneness of the life. The artist displayed a sense of loving awareness of various forms of life that surrounded him and unfolded the moving process of life itself by tying up vegetation, animals and birds life in the web of human existence.

2 The Hamza-Nama is a vision of the world through the eye of a lion. But a few scholars prefer to hold that Hamza-Nama was the brain child of Humayun. Beach, Milo C. *The Imperial Image painting for the Mughal Court*, Washington DC, 1981, p. 16.

i-Danish, Anwar-i-Suhaili, Humayun-Nama, Tuti-Nama, Ramayan, Nal-Damayanti, Laila-Majnun and other books have been illustrated and painted.

The illustrations to the Persian classical text generally followed and freely adapted with contemporary norms. In historical and biographical works, the painters fully utilised the opportunity to depict narrative scenes, thus providing valuable evidence of contemporary life to the art and social historians. All types of artist, materials and ingradients were made available to the painters.[1] Just as the painters have gained perfection in their work so have margin makers, book-binders, illuminators and gilders found themselves in great demands. In many examples the name of designer, the colourist and portrait painters are indicated. It is also possible to determine the style of master. In many instances these ascription carry such appellation as Kallan (Senior), Khurd or Chela (disciple) painting out their positions in Taswir Khana (Studio). In some cases, name of father, brother, teacher are also appended; and at the same time cities name are also found e.g. Lallu Lahori, Kesav Gujrati and Sur Gujrati, Bhim Gujrati, Nand Gwaliari, Ahmad Kashmiri; some foreigners names e.g. Mando Firangi and Bilal Habshi have also been found.

Example of joint productions with the outline designed by well known Master like Daswant,[2] Basawan, Kesav the

1 Ibid., p. 24.

2 The painting that shows Akbar slaying a tigress is actually the right half double pager painting in Akbar Nama. It is inscribed as 'tarah Basawan amal Tara Kalan' 'Chehra Basawan' which means composed by Basawan and painted by Tara the Elder and again face by Basawan.

elder, Lal, Miskin,[1] Ramdas etc. are common in the historical, biographical and religious works. The painters were a hereditary professionals as Muhammud Sharif and Bihzad, son of Khwaja 'Abd-us-Samad; Manohar son of Basawan; Govardhan son of Bhavanidas; Bisandas, nephew of Nanha; Daumar, brother of Daulat; the name of the teacher-Daulat disciple of Farrukh Beg, Nadira Banu, disciple of Aqa Reza are also indicated. A group of superbly produced manuscripts with exquisitely calligraphed text, elegant bindings and highly finished painting be selected group of master painters were produced. Illustrated manuscripts of legends and fables for example from Anwari-i-Suhaili, Iyar-i-Danish and Laila-wa-Majnun and visual narratives of hunting, bird trapping and animal fights contain truthful representations of animal nature, mood and behaviour. Each drawing imbed with the expression of ferocity, compassion, fear or bodily tension, specially noticed in the hunting and expedition scenes. In these works the miniatures were executed from designing to finishing by a single master. The art itself is exquisite, revealing not just a mastery of the craft but also details about way of life, costume, hunting styles and rituals throughout Mughal India.

Nevertheless, the one great characteristic of Mughal art which has distinguished it in the world's art is its closeness to nature. In fact a love of nature and love of art were the most absorbing passions of the Mughals. And the two went together, the former finding its fulfillment in art and the later its inspiration in nature. Flora and fauna, therefore, became subjects of their supremely poetic and artistic imagery, which together created in Mughal art a living world of beauty,

1 Miskin also contributed the painting of a lion courts with his skill hand (Pl. 5).

vibrating with life and feeling, and occasionally instinct with the same emotions and passion which govern human life. Love of nature was deeply marked trait of character. He had almost the same love of garden and flower which his grand father Babur possessed.

One of the most interesting of Akbar departments maintained was that of the animals. Akbar's interest in elephant almost verged on to infatuation. From boyhood when he was presented with a perfectly quiet elephant by his father, till the last days of his life when he watch some of his finest elephants in combat, his interest never waned. The Akbar Nama is full of reference to the elephants received by him as homage or booty from all over the country, trapped by him in the jungle of Central India or acquired through his nobles and officials. Abul-Fazl deals with elephants in his text, the *Ain-i-Akbari*, where every single detail about them was recorded including their classifications, upkeep food, kinds of staff appointed to train and look after them and an interesting comments on the Khass (special) elephant and how Akbar handled them, is described.[1] Illustrated elephants appeared either on biographical works (such as Akbar Nama) or as individual studies for mounting in an album. The depiction of elephants are also noticed in the historical, religious and literary manuscripts and every where, it has received equal care and attention, therefore, this animal found represented in *Dastan-i-Amir Hamza*,[2] in *Anwar-i-*

1 Abul Fazl, *A'in-i-Akbari*, tr. Into English by H. Blockmann, 1873, vol. I, pp. 123-129.

2 The elephant razing the fort to the ground in Hamza Nama folio preserved in the Bharat Kala Bhavan, Banaras Hindu University, Varanasi, has also been treated realistically in a purely Indian manner. It is imbued with almost human understanding and seems

Suhaili,[1] in *Rajm Nama, Ramayana, Babur Nama, Akbar Nama* and so on.

In Mughal India, trade, war, recreation and communication largely depended on horses. Therefore, Mughals prized them highly. Abdus Samad painted a large number of horses (Pl. 17). Akbar was fond of horses also and regarded this animal as of great importance in administration and expeditions of conquest. He therefore, paid much attention to every thing that was connected with horses. Abdus Samad's carrier if closely analyzed, one finds a transformation in him from Safavid Persian to a Mughal painter. In spite of his transition from Persian to a Mughal painter Abdus Samad developed certain formula which remains unchanged throughout his career. Perhaps the most typical of these trade marks, are his horses. From his Safavid 'Horse and groom' to his mughal ones, the features of Abdus Samad's horses remain constant. Their head are small and

---

to comprehend the grimness of the situation in the same manner as the furiously attacking soldier.

1 Bharat Kala Bhavan, Banaras Hindu University, Varanasi has in its collection an illustrated Persian manuscript of Akbari period dated 1596 A.D. This manuscript recently has been identified as the popular version of *Anwar-e-Suhaili* and is identified as *Iyar-e-Danish.* This being a Persian adoption of Sanksrit *Panchatantra* where animals play a very significant role. The manuscript has twenty five illustrations. Barring a few, most of the paintings bear the names of the painters. Painted at Lahore, the manuscripts were decorated with illustrations by famous Akbari painter namely Baswana, Miskin, Farrukh Chela, Jagannath, Mukund, Shankar, Dharmadas etc. (Pl. 4, 5, 6, 7, 9 & 12).

Farrukh Chela introduced in this painting human expression but at the same time, their inner characters were not forgotten altogether. It appears that Farrukh Chela studied the nature and movements of these wild animals from a close distance and as a result of which he could render them with evident naturalism (Pl. 4).

fine, their mouth are often open, as if neighing and their girths and hind quarters are disproportionately large in relation to their fore quarters. Dappled grey horses were favorites of Abdus Samad but dark skinned horses and even a pietbald mount figure was his oeuvre as well.[1]

---

1 Canby R. Shela, 'Mughal Masters : Further Studies', *Marg* (ed.) Asok Kumar Das, Vol. 49, No. 4, 1998, pp. 16-18.

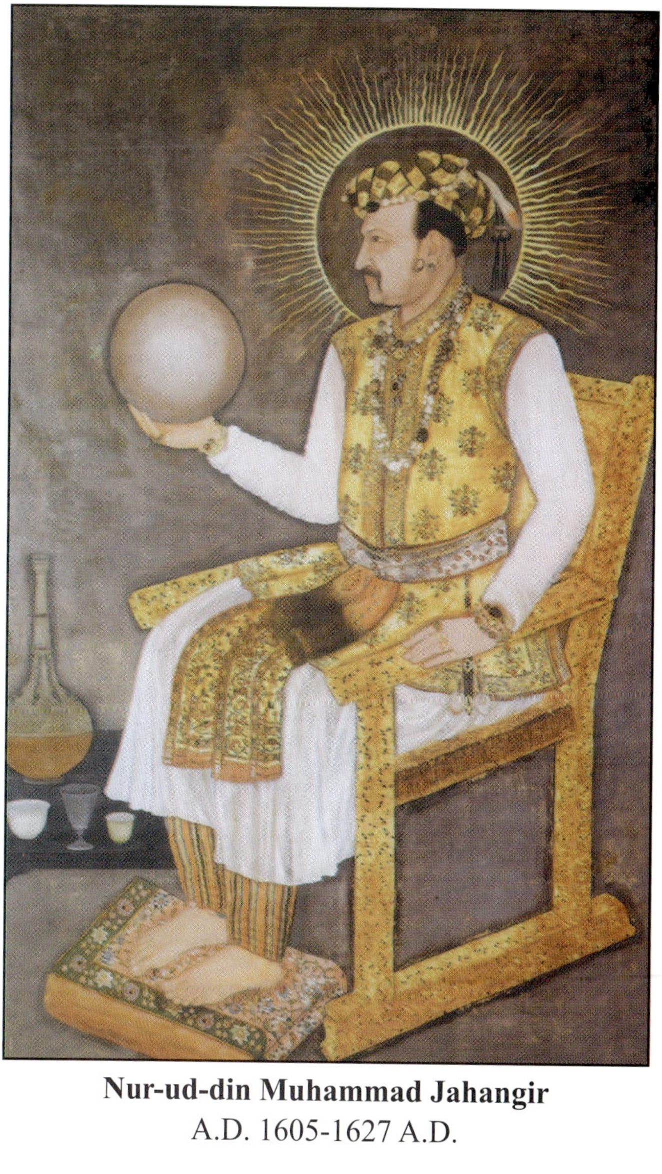

Nur-ud-din Muhammad Jahangir

A.D. 1605-1627 A.D.

After the death of Emperor Akbar, Salim ascended the throne in A.D. 1605 and was known as Jahangir. The years of Jahangir's reign from A.D. 1605 to 1627 A.D. were politically unremarkable. The foundation of Mughal rule in India by Babur, the period of unsettled fortune of Humayun, and spectacular success achieved in the battle filed and out side by Akbar, the period of Jahangir was little more than a colourless inter-regnum. Jahangir's easy-going nature proved no match for his father's excellences. However, Jahangir was neither a weakling nor an unworthy administrator and the basic political structure of enormous Mughal empire did not undergo any drastic change or reduction during his reign. The easygoing man Jahangir was more interested in game of polo, he was an aristocrat with the eye of a naturalist, the vision of poet, the taste of connoisseur and the outlook of an epicurean. He himself was a good calligraphist and had a great weakness for fine arts. He was keen lover of nature and art and his personality was reflected in the art and culture of their time.

Jahangir's deep and long lasting interest in painting, it is necessary to follow the activities of his art atelier started during his princely days as then he was called Salim. As a prince, he founded a small studio under the headship of a Harati painter Aqa Reza. Aqa Reza reached the Mughal court alongwtih Farruk Beg from Kabul. Aqa Reza and his other co-artist prepared miniatures and assembled albums (murraqqas) to mount the excellent collection of Persian and early Mughal paintings. Rare and valuable examples of calligraphic specimens from the pens of such famous calligraphers as Sultan Ali, and Mir Ali etc. were mounted on the large elegantly coloured folios. The borders (Hashiyas) of these folios were decorated with delicate drawings of the vegetal and floral patterns, combined with birds and animals. Gold was very much used in these decorations. Through these magnificent decorations it is possible to find out the emperor's liking and painter's delight to illustrate these. In these drawings signatures of artists such as – Aqa Reza Daulat, Bisandas, Govardhan, Balchand, Abu'l Hasan and Mansur, Bichitr and Hasim etc. have been found in margins. He himself monitored and supervised the work of his painters and encouraged them in a positive way of prosper. Therefore, result of such direct active patronage painting got a new vocabulary and different meanings. Though Jahangir did not invent any special script as his great grand father Babur did, neither he did care to know nor he could write good Nasta'liq., but he did not fail to recognize writers, learned teachers, poets. His handwriting, as appears on the fly-leaves of M.ss. and on miniatures from his collection, is not elegant but characteristically bold. His autobiography, the *Tuzuk*, offers a good account of his straight forward and rather naïve thoughts and ideas as well as penchant for small detail.

Jahangir followed in Babur foot-steps in observing and recording the beautiful flower and unusual fruit, and not only described them in detail but also instructed his painters to include their accurate likeness in *Jahangir-Nama*.[1] Like his great grandfather (Babur), he was keen lover of the beauties of nature and art. The *Tuzuk* of Jahangir records the wild animals, birds, garden plants of India and contains a sensitive account of gardens of Kashmir. It reveals Jahangir's love for nature. Jahangir's favourite artist was Mansur, some

1 *Tuzuk*, 1, 215-6; H.S. Hodivala, *Studies in Indo-Muslim History*, II, Bombay, 1957, pp. 316-17.

of whose early paintings are seen in the *Babur-Nama.*[1] Jahangir's character become more apparent when he is compared with his predecessors, especially with his great-grandfather Babur and his father Akbar. He inherited some notable traits from them, yet in some respects his character was almost the reverse of theirs.

As it has been already said that the Mughal school of painting had already been begun by his grand father Humayun and gradually developed as most successful school of art during Akbar's regime with new norms of painting which provided establishment to it. Now it was left to Jahangir to infuse new meaning, dimension and refinement into Mughal painting. With his critical mind, connoisseur's eye, sophisticated taste and penchant for details the paintings prepared under his patronage become remarkable for their refinement and quality. Therefore, to appreciate the character of the painting executed under Jahangir, it is necessary to realize his passionate love of nature, his joy in all wonders that the world held for him. Jahangir was born with the artistic and aesthetic temperament, which enabled him to admire all things in their most perfect state of beauty. Accordingly his whole nature throbs with ecstasy as he reveals in his gardens among flowers or under fruitful trees, listening to the music of the birds. All these he loved, and becomes an artist and a poet, and yearned to reproduce them in colour.

---

1 M.S. Randhawa, *Painting of Babur-Nama*, New Delhi, 1983. The *Babur-Nama* of National Museum (N.M. 50.326) New Delhi has 378 folios. Out of these 122 folios are illustrated with 144 illustration. The folios bear the name of 49 artists, neatly written by the calligrapher. Of these artists Mansur was the same who later on painted birds and animals for Jahangir and Daulat was an artist of high merit.

However, inspite of Jahangir's poetical temperament, which would cause him to remark of a perfume that 'it restores hearts that have gone and brings back withered souls', Mughal painting, in the hands of its actual exponents, remind intrinsically an art of prose, its acknowledged intention being frank realism, an effort to represent the object 'as in itself it really is'. In a word, Jahangir supplied the aesthetic fact that artists vision – while his court painters provided the physical fact – the externalization of that vision, the two co-operating to produce the actual work of art. In studying the painting of this period we shall see how the ideals of the emperor and the skill of craftsmen were combined in the highest attainment of the Mughal school. From this the conduct of his whole life testifies to his passion for every form of art, especially pictures.

Jahangir's own proficiency in this subject, especially of his knowledge of the individual mannerisms of the different artists, whether past or contemporary, is clear from his pronouncement– 'As regard myself', my liking for painting and my practice in judging it have arrived at such a point that when any work is brought to me, either deceased artists' or those of the present day, without the name being told me, I can say that it is the work of such and such an artist. And if there be a picture containing many portraits, and each face be the work of a different master, I can discover which face is the work of whom. If any other person has put in the eye and eyebrow of a face; I can perceive whose work the original face is, and who has painted the eyes and eyebrows.' It certainly describes Jahangir as something more than a close observer of each of artists method of work.[1] It is quite

1 Such a system of production seems to suggest that the painting of Mughal school was more of a craft than of a fine art. It seems that

clear that his knowledge of painting was not that of a mere dilettante, but that of an experienced connoisseur. Jahangir was an antiquarian with an artist's eye, and out of well spring of his knowledge he supplied this missing quality, using it with rare judgment, as the art of his time bear eloquent testimony.

His reign, on the whole, was fruitful of peace and prosperity to the empire. Under his auspices the industry and commerce progressed, architecture achieved notable triumphs, painting reached its high water mark, literature flourished as never before. In his memoirs, known as the *Tuzuk-i-Jahangiri* or *Jahangir-Nama*, fascinating, day to day account of his life and of his perception of nature and art with meticulous details were recorded. He was a lover of beauty be it that of an artifact or that observed in nature. When artist produced something unique, he rewarded him and bestowed honour upon him. Artists and craftsmen, builder and architects, calligrapher and engravers hold high position in court. Keeping pace with the emperors demand for objects of unknown brilliance and impeccable quality, the artists and craftsmen of Jahangir India strove hard to create new conventions.

Emperor Jahangir's vivid and accurate description of several birds and animals undoubtedly present him as a keen observer of nature and indicate his desire for realistic expression. Not satisfied with textual description, he ordered

---

the painters were assembled in a workshop, and there, under a head artist, each was executing those parts of the painting with which he was most familiar. The actual composition of the miniature would be sketched by the chief artist, then one artist drawing the figures another painting the background, a third putting in the features and so on, until each had completed the portion of the work allotted to him and the whole was finished. By such means any body get a superlative work of art. It also proved that such a method of partnership was common by the Emperor Jahangir's comment.

his painters to draw likenesses. Jahangir considered pictorial representation as a source of amazement, recognized the importance of the documentation of rarities[1] to be passed on to later generations. Consequently, numerous studies of birds and animals were made by his painters. These pictures display simpler composition accommodating the central theme, probably to allow maximum details. One can not fail to admire the minute observation of the artists in which other characteristics, physical features of various birds and animals are realistically depicted so as to enable one to identify the species at first glance. The depiction in natural surroundings further enhance the lively effect. After careful study, examining the object closely the artist painted them, their creations not appeared merely as a copy. It is noted that Jahangir was not so interested about elephants as Akbar was. In spite of all Jahangir examined the nature of an elephant with the interest of a zoologist. He carefully noted their behaviour and recorded their gestation period. It is also interesting to note that many of his favourite elephants were painted by his artists. Their names and details were recorded by the emperor.

Among the host of painters working under Jahangir, Farrukh Beg, Daulat, Manohar, Bisandas, Mansur and Abu-l-Hasan secured their artistic genius when entered into the Akbari atelier during its hey day but each developed his individualistic style which was never submerged in the milieu of its syncretistic atmosphere. Daulat, Manohar, Bisandas and Mansur all worked during the last few years of Akbar's reign as budding masters. From a fragmentary inscription on

1 Jahangir's most valuable contribution to the knowledge of Zoology was a portrait of the Mauritian bird, the Dodo. This flightless, primitive bird had become extinct by the end of 17th century.

a miniature of the Nafahat-al-Une in the British Museum, we come to know that Daulat was pupil of Farrukh Beg. Manohar, son of celebrated Akbari master Basawan and Bishandas, nephew of another Akbari painter Nanha excelled in portrait painting. Apart from above artist some superb miniatures were painted by Bichitra, Hashim, Govardhan, Inayet, Murad, Padarath, Balchan, Aqa Reza were also most important artist of Jahangiri court. The most important of all Jahangiri painters were Ustad Mansur and Abu-l-Hasan. The emperor himself speaks highly of them and bestowed the titles Nadir-al-Asra and Nadir-uz-Zaman on them respectively in recognition of their merit. Mansur started his carrier during the last few years of Akbar's reign as a minor painter but due to Jahangir's profound personal interest, he became an incomparable expert of drawing of natural history subjects. His studies of rare animals, uncommon birds, unusual flowers etc. are also meticulous and lively that ornithologists wonder at his scientific power of observation. Mansur reflect his great confidence in his brush and in depth of his vision and spontaneity of or precision in the study of birds. Two signed works of this great master-one of the rare Siberian crane and the other of a Bengal florican are in the Indian Museum, Calcutta, while some more may be found in the National Museum, New Delhi, and Maharaja Sawai Man Singh II Museum, Jaipur and Prince of Wales Museum, Bombay. Abu-l-Hasan was a far more sophisticated painter who was born within the Mughal household, and was equally proficient in all branches of miniature painting but the most interesting feature of his works is the colour scheme, very effective, very attractive and colourful. The extraordinary painting of a Chinar tree with hosts of squirrels in every conceivably position evince his acumen. Abu-l-Hasan has painted the spirit as well as the outer forms one can almost hear the chatter of birds and animals frightened by the approach of the fowler in his composition of the Chinar tree. Abu-l-Hasan secured their artistic genius when entered into Akbari atelier during the last few years of Akbar's reign as budding master. The most important of all Jahangiri painters were Abu-l-Hasan also. And was equally proficient in all branches of miniature painting but most interesting feature of his works is the colour scheme, very effective, very attractive and colourful. The extraordinary painting of a Chinar tree with hosts of squirrels in every conceivably position evince his acumen. Abu-l-Hasan has painted the spirit as well as the outer form. One can almost here the chatter of birds and animals (Pl. 18). Emperor Jahangir had all praise for painter Abul Hasan above other painters of his time but in his memoir Jahangir mentions Mansur frequently. Based on the natural history, the painting of animal and birds are best known in the works of Ustad Mansur. Most probably he received the title 'Ustad' during Akbar's life time. Mansur's career can be traced from Akbar's times.[1] He painted animals

1 Geeti Sen, *Painting from the Akbarnama*, Calcutta, 1984, p. 147, pl. 65. Mansur who became a celebrated painter in Jahangir's time made a number of animal and birds studies, sometimes jointly and at times alone. In *Akbarnama* (Ca. 1590-1595 A.D.) of Victoria and Albert Museum, London, there is a double page composition showing the great hunt near Lahore in 1567; the drawing of the left half of this composition was done by Basawan and was painted by Mansur while the right half was drawn by Basawan and painted by Hussain Naqqash. Of the same manuscript, mention may be made of a painting showing Husain Quli Khan presents prisoners of war from Gujarat before Akbar. The left half of this double page painting was drawn by Basawan and painted by Mansur. This painting of Victoria and Albert Museum shows prisoners sewed upto animal hides of a cow, a buffalo, a camel, a bear, a monkey, a sambhar, a black buck and cheetah.

and birds in *Babar Nama*, in *Akbar Nama* and in *Changiz Nama*. He worked there as a Chela (Junior artist) to some of the first Mughal master like – Basawan, Miskin, Kanha and Nanha but in the second version of *Akbar Nama*, he worked independently. His talents were recognized and he received imperial attention in his painting in *Akbar Nama* and *Babur Nama*. A number of early manuscript illustrations are found painted by Mansur but were not designed by him which means that he was not immediately recognized as a Major artist. An illustrated *Babur Nama* page of 1590-95 in the Frur Gallery of Art, Washington was designed by Kanha and painted by Mansur shows his early style fully formed.

The Mughal painters took inspiration from various trends of art, even before Jahangir, the long tradition of manuscript painting, illustrating fables and legends both in Persia and Mughal court, provided artists an opportunity to become acquainted with animal's characters and behaviour. A large number of pictures of birds and animals, mostly ascribed to Abu-l-Hasan, Goverdhan, Inayet, Mansur, Murad and Padarath of Jahangir Studio have survived (Pl. 18, 19-26).

Jahangir's contribution to the art appears to have more significant for painting than towards that of architecture. He was keen lover of nature and art and was endowed with an aesthetic sensibility. Another important development took place during Jahangir periods which led to change in the style of Mughal painting. The trend started in his princely days, was vigorously pursued by Jahangir and Mughal painting reached its logical culmination in the course of his reign. He helped it to be free from its bond with the text of manuscripts as it was his desire to have a small group of master painters, each highly specialized in one or more branches of art, who could prepare of persons on groups or themes selected by him and pulsating with life.

Towards the end of his life the light of his happiness was dimmed. Jahangir feasted his eyes on its many delights, but his strength was failing. He died in the year 1627 A.D. with his passing the soul of Mughal painting also departed; its outward form remained for a time under the other kings, but its real spirit died out with Jahangir. Artist and nature-worshipper to the end, his last words were characteristic of the men, 'Let my tomb lie open to the winds of haven, so that the rain and dew may fall on it'; it is the school of painting which so perfectly reflected his artistic nature and which, imbued with this spirit, was stimulated to its finest achievements.

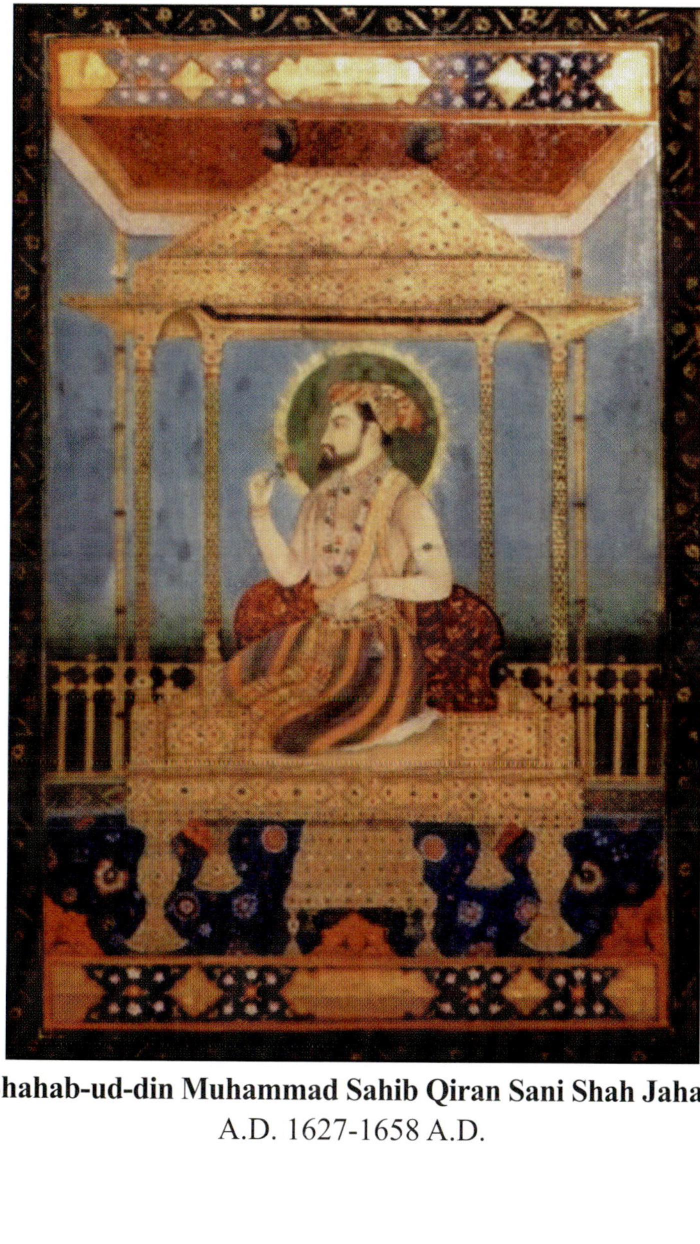

Shahab-ud-din Muhammad Sahib Qiran Sani Shah Jahan
A.D. 1627-1658 A.D.

Shah Jahan ascended the Mughal throne on 24th January 1928 A.D. In the course of his long rule, Shah Jahan largely transformed the form and content of Mughal painting and took away much of its creativeness and only occasional sparks are discernible in the limited production of the imperial atelier. But the relation that existed between Jahangir and his court painters were not continued by his successor Shah Jahan, nevertheless his reign was one of remarkable artistic activity. His artistic patronage did not specially confine itself to painting, as did Jahangir's; it was more comprehensive, and diffused itself over the whole filed of the fine arts and applied arts. All kind of decorative arts metalware, wood carving, glass, lapidary work, textile and carpet weaving received his attentation as a result of which the richest brocades, finest Jades, costliest thrones and jewellery and embroidered stuffs were produced in his time. With the result, not only that one but all the crafts and arts were flourished. This emperor name is, however, chiefly associated with architecture, because it is by the many noble buildings erected in his reign that he is widely known. He embellished old structures with white marble, built new forts and masques. He clothed the robustness of Akbari creations with beauty and poetic grace. He spent much of his energy and wealth to build a befitting mausoleum for his beloved wife Mumtaj Mahal, remains to this day an unique edific of the rarest class which made him immortal in the world. The paintings obviously lack the personal touch and attentation of an art loving patron like his father Jahangir.

At the beginning of Shah Jahan reign, there was a little change in the course of miniature painting; artist stayed on in the imperial employ and continued to paint in the same styles. Shahjahan's interest in painting were never as involved as those of his father; however, there is hardly any indication that he participated in creating them as did Jahangir. The protocol that dominated the courts functions is easily discernible in imperial painting. Works generally became more linear as well as more meticulous, and it is possible to compare the coolness of his picture, the pristine white marble he used for construction or the gems he prized. He seems to have viewed painting purely as a decorative art and therefore, did not require the same expressiveness from his miniaturists as did Jahangir.

As a prince, Shah Jahan was interested in painting like his father Jahangir. Shah Jahan was not only a great builder of beautiful monuments but also a passionate nature worshipper. A love of nature was a grand imperial heritage among the Mughals. The unusual, the picturesque and the graceful in nature, whether in flora or fauna, invariably aroused the admiration and emotions of the rulers which caused in them an urge to discover the joys of the senses in art. There was not dearth of talented persons in their court who know how to diffuse the lyrical moods and emotions of their patrons in beautifully rhythmic forms breathing life. And so, we find the zeal of the emperors and the skill of their artists combining to bring about the perfect conditions in which to create enchanting world of nature in the most vivid forms. Shah Jahan was the 'Great Grand Mughal of India, in the radiant sphere his court was to be found splendor flashing with gold, elegance touched with sensuousness, a kingliness characterized by fastidiousness. All this was reflected in the cultural expressions of the Shah Jahan period.

In the filed of art Shah Jahan's passion was building in which he indulged to the utmost. He continued the traditions undisturbed but Shah Jahan was more interested in architecture, precious stones and jewellery. The art of Shah Jahan is also noteworthy for the influence of painting on architectural decoration. Hashiyas (border) as a form of embellishment in Mughal miniatures had been specially developed by the artists of Jahangir. They were superb works of art in themselves and gave the miniatures a gorgeousness hitherto unknown. They had naturally an impact on the mind of the architectural decorator. Therefore, the counterpart of the Hashiya decorations of the Diwan-i-Khas and other buildings of this period. Floral beauties with their stems and leaves in harmonizing tones of green were no doubt carved on the main places, but around these in broad borders ran floral scrolls which were decorated with an inlay of precious stones, sometimes the colour and design being exactly the same as in the miniatures. E.B. Havell brought to our notice, border of few Mughal paintings, done in the time of Jahangir, the floral designs of which are exactly similar to the Hashiya decoration in the Taj.[1]

It has already been said that as a prince, Shah Jahan was interested in painting like his father Jahangir. He also started his own atelier and built up a collection of paintings consisting of portraits, genre scene, European engravings and the like. An album consisting of these materials alongwith panels of his own calligraphic exercise, done between 1608 and 1617, has survived. However, albums formed by him after his accession generally contains formal portraits of his noble and officials, and only occasional studies of birds and animals. But unlike Jahangir, whose idea on painting differed from those of his father, Shah Jahan encouraged artists to continue painting as they had for his father. His

1 E.B. Havell, *Essays on Indian Art, Industry and Education*, pp. 17-18, *Journal of Indian Art and Industry*.

pictures, therefore, are sometimes difficult to differentiate from Jahangirs, although colours tend to be more jewel-like, and their mood is usually more restrained. Inspite of all the Mughal style of miniature painting which had reached its climax under Jahangir, appeared under Shah Jahan mainly as a means of gorgeous depiction of the pomp and glitter of court life with all its sumptuous paraphernalia. The artist do not show that keen interest in animals and birds life as they did in Jahangir's time, and individual plants and flowers rarely engage their attention in paintings.

Shah Jahan took no pleasure in the production of his official painters, perhaps he had not that passion for pictures which was notable characteristic of his predecessors. He maintained his staff a limited and select body of highly trained artists, in number these were nothing to be compared with the great concourse of painters who for over a generation had been dependent on the patronage of the Mughal rulers. The group of painters who had flocked around Akbar's and Jahangir's courts, finding their services no longer required under the new reign. The tradition continued in the time of Shah Jahan, now it was touched by an increased sense of richness and elegance which sometimes made one mess the originality and vitality of earlier period.

The tradition of making Muraqqas continued during Shahjahan's time. The border decoration along the four sides of the miniature contained floral scrolls and arabesques in the midst of which human, animal and bird figures are also present. One such painting has Muhammad Faquirullah Khan, head artist of the court of Shahjahan, as the central theme. The border on the left has two lines of flowering plants in the middle of which there are three standing human figures. The upper and lower margins have only one row each of flowering plants with men sitting among both representations of flora in margins done during Shahjahans period seems to have received only a place of secondary importance because human figures dominate the landscape. Compared to Jahangirs paintings those of Shahjahan appear dull and ponderous. The paintings produced during the reign of Shahjahan period are noted for their refinement and meticulous execution. The illuminated calligraphic folios exemplify the elaborate border style of the period. An element of stiffness permeates such finished works of the era, which demonstrate the decline of the spontaneity and the flow of the earlier period.

The most important product of his reign is the *Padshah Nama* manuscript at present in the Royal Library at the Windstor castle, like his grandfather Akbar, he entrusted his court historian to record the official account of his reign. When Muhammad Amir Qaziwine completed the account of the first ten years of his reign, Shah Jahan gave this task to 'Abd ul Hamid Lahori to rewrite it according to the lunar years of the Hijri Calendar in place of Persian solar reckoning followed by Qaziwine. Lahori completed the first part of his *Padshah Nama* consisting the account of the first decade by June, 1641A.D., the second part by November, 1648 A.D. and the last volume partly compiled by Muhammad was done by December, 1657 A.D. The Windsor castle manuscript of the first volume of *Padshah Nama* was copied in 1106-7H/1656-57A.D. and contains forty four illustrations. These paintings are very different from the illustrations of the *Jahangir Nama* and painted in a stiff formal style. The painting took much care to show rich furnishings, floor spreads and dazzling jewels, and princes and courtiers wearing elaborate costumes standing in rows or orderly processions of caparisoned elephants and horses with musicians and performers. These painting obviously lack the personal touch of an art loving patron like Jahangir.

The Windsor manuscript contains signed works of Balchand, Lalchand, Ramdas, Murad, Bichitr, Bhola, Abid, Payag and Mirdost all leading painters of the times. The borders of the folios of these albums often contain fine drawings of flowering plants and birds in multy colour within delicate geometrical and vegetal designs in gold.

Shah Jahan was interested in portraiture. Initially experiencd painters like Govardhan, Abul Hasan, Hashim and Bichitr prepared these lively portraits. Gradually Balchand, Murad, Payag, Chitraman, Manohar, Lal Chand and Abid specialized in this branch and painted many wonderful portraits.

The painting of Shahjahan seated on a golden throne holding a prize falcon on his gloved hand given by his eldest son Dara Shikoh, who is standing before him is a superb example of such portrait studies. It bears the signature of the veteran painter Govardhan who specialised as a portraitist early in Jahangir reign.

A number of gorgeous pictures of the court of Shahjahan, with its pomp and magnificence, contain some very fine studies of animals and birds. A Darbar scene shows Ali Mardana Khana, governor of Qandhar or Qandahar, paying homage to the Emperor. Among the presents he brought for Shahjahan, include gaily caparisoned horses, for which western Asia was famous in those times. In the foreground of the picture there are at least nine of theme and these appear as sleek and powerful animals of noble strain. Although standing, their exquisite forms do not hide the quality of swift limbs which has probably been more successfully brought out here than in the galloping horses of *Babur Nama* and *Akbar Nama*. Their long arched necks with wiry strands of hair, full and soft eyes, their aristocratic heads and their delicate slender bodies make it easy to identity them. Physically, they are the prized Arab horses, and artistically, they are the Indianised Persian types.

Single studies of a number of animals and birds were also made during the reign of Shahjahan. The Emperor possessed a pink elephant, which was made the subject of study in a painting, now in American collection. It is the picture of a magnificent beast which was evidently a Royal show piece. Although its enormous bulk is not very elegantly proportioned, its august dignity is deeply emphasized by its bejeweled coverings, pearl tassels and golden bells. But perhaps the ornamental prappings were not considered sufficient to establish its stateliness. It is mounted by Dara Shikoh, the most favoured son of the Emperor, and preceded by a groom who holds the royal standard marked with the figure of a golden lion. The elephant, no doubt, is fully aware of the honour shown to it as its smiling expression suggests pleasure and its bright eye in view is softly fixed on the viewer. It is believed on stylistic grounds that this portrait of the elephant was painted by Bichitr, one of the most brilliant artists of the 17th century. He was a sensitive and accurate observer whose characterization are endowed with majestic solidity.

Another fine study of an elephant is in the Victoria and Albert Museum. This too is mounted by the young Prince Dara and is very grandly caparisoned. The ornamental textile covering is adorned with tulip flowers formally arranged. From the writing on the painting it appears that the name of the elephant was Mahaparbat. Its physical proportions are not flattering but there is a touch of a regal majesty in the elephants swinging motions as it moves onwards.

Another study of elephant of Shahjahan period, the artist of which is unknown, is in the Prince of Wales Museum, Bombay. Chained elephants had been the subject of study previously as well; but here the artists has succeeded remarkably well in contrasting the blustering rhythm of the massive black form which is continually in motion with the subdued background which consists of the dry trunk and leafless branches of a tall tree on which very small birds are quietly sitting.

'Neelgai' is one more animal study belonging to the closing year of Shahjahan's reign. It is now in the Prince of Wales Museum, Bombay. Its form is realistically rendered, but it rather lacks the quality of sensitive characterization seen in the zoological portraitures of the previous regime.

Shahjahan continued the tradition of hunting. One painting shows him slaying a lion in the presence of his father near Agra in 1611 A.D., while another, probably from 1632 A.D., shows him alongwith Dara Shikoh, Shah Suja and Aurengzeb, shooting a lioness while a lioness snarls at one of the elephants. Two of her cubs are also seen in the painting. The *Shahjahan Nama* of Inayet Khan records several instances of hunting black buck; a miniature of the *Padashah Nama* showing the royal entourage on the move from Lahore to Agra in the 8th regnal year, shows a Cheetah being carried on a bullock cart.

Shahjahan and his son Dara Shikoh also showed interest in this subject and many remarkably drawings of birds, animals and flowers were made during this period. Some of these are preserved in the album compiled by Prince Dara Shikoh for his wife. A number of drawings based on earlier works of Mansur, Inayet, Abul Hasan etc. were prepared by the painters of the Shahjahan's atelier.

Owing to illness and age, the hand of emperor Shahjahan began to relinquish its holds on the affairs of the empire, the art, too, had reached its first stage of dissolution.

Shahjahan's eldest son Dara Shikoh took keen pleasure in pictures. This gifted prince was a collector of these works of art, as is proved by a precious album of miniatures bearing his signature and now in the India Office Library, London.[1] Prince Dara Shikoh carried on his grandfather's interest in natural history and we have some beautiful fauna studies in the album of the Prince including a pair of ducks, now preserved in the India Office Library, London. One of these is the drawing of a pair of ducks in clour. Although the artist is not known, the drawing reminds us of the magic of Mansur's delicate strokes which evidently continued to enchant the artists of the succeeding generations. The whole is a picturesque scene of wild bird-life. The side of the pool at the foot of the hillock over which can be seen the distant outline of clearly defined branches and leaves of trees, and flying birds fluttering in the sky, serve as the background for the magnificently featured birds. But it is the expert handling of the brush with which the painter deftly suggested solidity and roundness and expressed the forms in all their exquisite details, noticing even the faint hint of the tender pressure of the birds webbed feed on the ground that makes this one of the best bird studies of the entire Mughal atelier.

From the same album, we have the picture of a handsome and elegant Night Heron. Its sharp and dagger-like beak, its large eyes and the retracted neck, as well as its

1 Percey Brown, *Indian Painting under the Mughal*, Oxford, 1924, London, p. 94.

bent legs have been very realistically rendered. Indeed this painting and the pervit the hawk and the jungle-cock all is in Prince of Wales Museum, Bombay, bear irrefutable evidence of the fact that the brilliance of Mansur's achievements still persisted in the time of Shahjahan. And the artists deeply penetrating insight into the habits and life of the birds we have them as beautifully executed as the other birds studies of the previous reign.

Dara Shikoh album contains studies of a bustard, a night heron, a drake, a pair of pigeons, two drakes, a pair of pheasant and two partridge, all uninscribed, but in the tradition of the great natural history painter Ustad Mansur. The study of the Himalyan Cheer Pheasant is directly derived from the picture of this bird in the wantage Album in the Victoria and Albert Museum, London, bearing the signature of Ustad Mansur. It closely resembles the painting of the same subject.

Dara Shikoh was also interested in paintings and following the current court custom got a murraqqa of portraits and miscellanea completed. This superb album assembled between A.D. 1633 to 1642 A.D. is bond in black morocco with a parel of red morocco having a design of strap work and flowers stamped in gold. The name of only one painter, Muhammad Khan, is found in this album of seventy two folios, now preserved in India Office Library and Records, London. It contains illuminations, calligraphic specimen and sixty eight miniature of birds, flowers, flowering plants, young prince and beautiful princes etc.

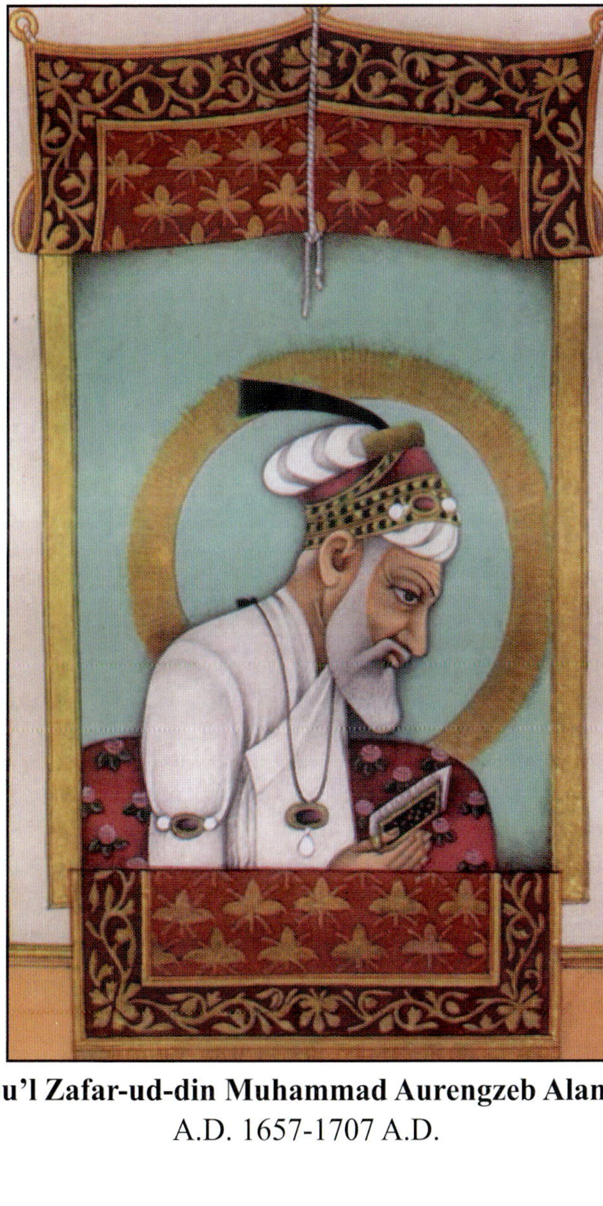

Abu'l Zafar-ud-din Muhammad Aurengzeb Alamgir
A.D. 1657-1707 A.D.

Shah Jahan was deposed by his third son Aurangzeb, who took the title of 'Alamgir' (seizer of universe) in the year 1658 A.D. Within hundred years, extending from the middle of the sixteenth century to middle of the seventeenth century, cover the whole period during which the Mughal school was a living art. From now begins the story of its decay. To Aurangzeb's unsympathetic policy the decline of the Mughal empire has been ascribed, to his puritanical personality to death of all kinds of art is attributed. After imprisoning his father whom he assumed the throne, his religious purity and thoughtfulness on a personal level, his policies tore down what his predecessors had built. Aurangzeb policies were the most destructive to the empire as well as art and craft too and he must share both credit and discredit for his policies,[1] at least to a very large extent. It was not merely the fall of an empire but also the end of an epoch. Aurengzeb was not a political genius and lacked the qualities of a true statesman who could initiate a policy and enact laws for moulding the life and thought of his contemporaries as well of future generations. He could realize the futility of his work before his death. His reign from A.D. 1658 to 1707 A.D. was turbulent marked by political chaos and cultural stagnation. Imperial patronage of art in the Mughal court declined, compelling artists to seek employment elsewhere in local court in provinces. Aurengzeb gave little encouragement to his people in the sphere of art, on the contrary that the arts generally flourshed very much as they did under his less bigotted predecessors. A miniature painting is a case in point. The number of paintings that were produced during the latter half of the seventeenth century, although undoubtedly

1 Jadunath Sarkar, *The Fall of Mughal Empire*, (In four volumes), New Delhi, 1950 & 1966.

inferiors in quality, was that many of these painting were executed with the emperor's concurrence, is shown by the fact that they often include a portrait of Aurengzeb himself. Where we see him hunting traveling, reading, governing and commanding his army, exactly as Jahangir and Shah Jahan were depicted in the miniatures of their times.

A few of the best Mughal paintings were made for Aurengzeb, perhaps, the artists realized that he might close the workshop and therefore, executed themselves on his behalf. For whatever reasons, this darbar is of stunning quality. The awesomely dignified emperor holds a hawk, while seated on an elegantly unpretentious gold throne beneath a canopy adorned with birds of paradise.

In the collection of Chester Beatty Library, Dublin, there is a large hunting scene that can hardly be bettered in seventeenth century Mughal art, even though it was painted for Aurengzeb, who virtually closed down the royal workshops a few years after he came to the throne. It was probably painted by Bichitr, the great master who had worked for Jahangir and Shah Jahan earlier (Pl.33A&B).

An album of bird and animal studies of Aurengzeb reign preserved in the Maharaj Sawai Man Singh II Museum, and it has several animals represented in it.

With the death of the Emperor Aurengzeb in 1707 A.D. the story of Mughal art and painting begins to draw to a close. To the last, in absence of tutelage and encouragement from the Delhi court, artists migrated towards provincial patrons. Mughal art, just like the Mughal Empire is marked by its rise, development, maturity, decadence and disintegration.

Names of Painters of the Great Mughals

Humayun

Mir Sayyid Ali & Khwaja Abdus Samad, both were disciple of Bihzad (Persian artist). Humayun brought them over from Tabriz to India. After Humayun's death, these artists played a major role in development of the art of painting at the Mughal court during the Akbar's reign.

Akbari Painters

Abdullha	Dhan Raj
Anant	Dhannu
Allha Quli	Durga
Asi (brother of Miskin)	Dharma Das
Asi Kahar	Dev Gujrati
Babu Naqqash	Farrukh Beg
Bhag	Farrukh Chela
Bandi	Govind
Banwari Kalan	Husain Naqqash
Banwari Khurd	Haribans
Basawan	Ikhlas
Bhawani	Ibrahim Naqqash
Bhawani Kalan	Ibrahim Kahar
Bhagwan	Jagan/Jagnath
Bhura	Jamal
Chitra Mani	Jagjiwan
Daswant	Jamshed
Daulat	Keheman
SangtarashKhusra Quli	Naman

Khem Karan
Khizra Khela
Kesu Gujrati
Kesu Kalan
Kanha
Lachhman
Lal
Muklas
Madhu Kalan
Makra
Mukund
Miskin
Mahesh
Madhu Khurd
Madhav
Mansur
Muhammad Kashmiri
Manohar
Nand Gwaliari
Narayan
Nand or Nandi (son of Ramdas)

Narsingh
Nanha
Nand Gwaliari
Paras
Param ji Gujrati
Qutub Chela
Ramdas
Sanwala
Sarwan
Surdas
Surjan
Shankar
Shivdas
Tulsi
Tulsi Kalan
Tara
Tiriya

Jahangiri Painters

Mansur

Abu-l-Hasan

Farrukh Beg

Daulat (Chela of Farrukh Beg)

Manohar (Son of Basawan)

Bisandas (Nephew of Nanha)

Bichitr

Hashim

Govardhan

Inayet

Murad

Padarath

Balchand

Aqa Reza

Nanha

Shah Jahani Artists

Payag

Balchand

Murad

Chitraman

Lal Chand

Abid

Ramdas

Bhola

Mir dust or Mir dost

Manohar

Muhammed Faquirullah Khan

Bichitr Hashim Abul Hasan Govardhan	These four painter of Jahangiri period also work for Shah Jahan.

The name of only on painter, Muhammad Khan, is found who work for Dara Shikoh.

Aurengzeb

In the collection of Chester Beatty Library, Dublin, there is a large hunting scene that can hardly be bettered 17th century Mughal art, even though it was painted for Aurengzeb, who virtually closed down the royal workshop after he came to the throne. It was probably painted by Bichitr, the great master who had worked for Jahangir and Shahjahan earlier.

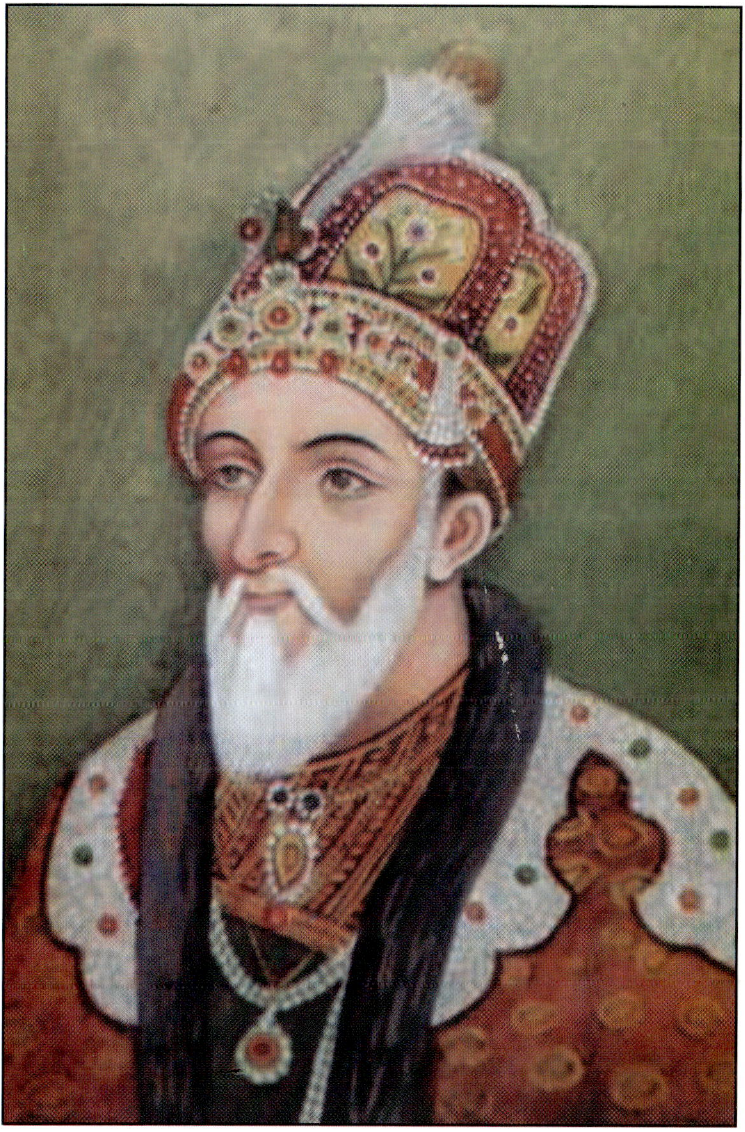

Last Mughal Emperor Bahadur Shah 'Zafar'

Bibliography

1. *Ain-i-Akbari,* Abul-Fazl trans. into English by H. Blochman, Edt. By S.L. Goomer, 2nd Ed. Delhi 1965.

   Abul-Fazl trans. Blochmann, Vol. 1, Calcutta, 1873.
2. Alvi, M.A. and Rahman, A., *Jahangir the Naturalist*, New Delhi, 1968.
3. Babar, *Babur-nama* (Memoirs of Babur), translated from orgiintal Turki text of Zahirid-din Muhammad Babur Padshah Gazi by Annett Susannah Beveridge, Vol. I and II, New Delhi, Reprinted, 1970.
4. Beach, Milo C., *The Grand Mughal · Imperial Painting in India 1600-1660*, U.S.A., 1978.

   The Imperial Image Painting for the Mughal Court, Washington DC, 1981.
5. Beni Prasad, *History of Jahangir*, Allahabad, 1962.
6. Brown, Percy, *Indian Painting under Mughals,* Oxford, 1924.
7. Chand, Moti, *Technique of Mughal Painting*, Lucknow, 1949.
8. Chandra,Pramod,Tuti-nama-TahsofaParrot,Commentarium, Graz. 1976.

9. Das, Asok Kumar, *Dawn of Mughal Painting*, Bombay, 1982.

Mughal Painting During Jahangir's Time, Calcutta, 1978.

Splendor of Mughal Painting, Bombay, 1986.

'Imperial Cheetahs in Akbar's Shikarkhana', the *Indian Magazine*, Vol. V, New Delhi, 1985.

'The Turkey in Mughal and Amber and Jaipur painting', *Journal of Indian Museum*, Vol. XXX & XXXI, Delhi, 1975.

Master Mughal Further studies, Mumbai, 1998

10. Divyabhanu Singh, *The End of A Trail*, Bombay, 1995.

11. Gascoigns, B., *The Great Mughal*, London, 1971.

12. Gosswamy, B.N., *Essence of Indian Art*, 1986.

13. Hodivala, H.S., *Studies in Indo-Muslim History*, II, Bombay, 1957.

14. Ishwari Prasad, *Life and Time of Humayun*, London, 1955.

15. Khandalawala, Karl J., 'Early Mughal', *Lalit Kala* Portfolio, No. 10, 1978.

16. *Marg*, Vol. 49, No. 4, 1998 and Vol. 50, No. 3, 1999.

17. Majumdar, R.C. (ed.), *The Mughal Empire*, Bombay, 1974.

18. Mehta, N.C., *Studies in Indian Paintings*, Bombay, 1926

19. Okada, Amina, *Imperial Munghal Painter*, Paris, 1992.

Indian Miniature of the Mughal Court, New York, 1992.

20. Pal, Pratapaditya, *Court-Painting of India*, New Delhi, 1983.

Master Artists of the Mughal Court, Marg Publication, Bombay, 1991.

21. Pinder Wilson, R.H., *Painting from Muslim Courts of India*, London, 1976.
22. Randhawa, M.S., *Painting of the Babur-Nama*, New Delhi, 1983.

    Ropa-Lakha, Vol. XLII, NO. I & II, p. 14.
23. Rai Krishnadas, *Anwar-e-Suhali* (Iyer-i-Danish), Varanasi, 1999.
24. Rogers, J.M., *Mughal Miniatures*, London, 1993.
25. Saksena, B.P., *Shah Jahan of Delhi*, Allahabad, 1932.
26. Sen, Geeti, *Painting from the Akbarnama*, Varanasi, 1984.
27. Sarkar, J.N., *The Fall of Mughal Empire*, London & Calcutta, 1912-1930.
28. Swarup Santi, *Flora and Fauna*, Bombay, 1983.
29. *Tuzuk-i-Jahangiri* or Memoirs of Jahangir, translated by Alexander Rogers edt. By Henry Beveridge, 2nd edition, Delhi, 1968.
30. *Tuzuk-i-Jahangiri*, Persian Text, edited by – Sayyed Ahmad, Gazipur and Aligarh, 1863-64.
31. Verma, Some Prakash, *Painting of Akbar's Court*, New Delhi, 1978; *Mughal Painters and Their Work, a Biographical Survey and Comprehensive Catalogue*, New Delhi, 1978.
32. Welsh, Stuart Carey, *Imperial Mughal Painting*, New York, 1978; India, Art and Culture, New York, 1986; The Art of Mughal, New York, 1963
33. Wells, H.G., *The Outline of History*, London, 1930.

Index

A

Abd ul Hamid Lahori 67
Abd-us-Samad 35, 40, 44
Abdus Samad 35, 46, 47, 79
Abdus Samad painted 46
Abid 68, 82
Abul Fazl 41, 42, 45
Abu-l-Hasan 52, 56, 57, 58, 59, 81
Abul Hasan 58, 68, 71, 82
aesthetic 53, 54, 59
Afghanistan 22, 24
Agra 70
Ahmad Kashmiri 43
Ain-i-Akbari 45
Ajanta 19
Akbar 21, 22, 23, 24, 28, 35, 36, 37, 39, 40, 41, 42, 43, 45, 46, 51, 53, 56, 57, 58, 59, 66, 67, 69, 79
Akbari 23
Akbari atelier 56, 58
Akbari creations 63
Akbari painter 46, 57
Akbari period 46
Akbar-Nama 22
Akbar's school of painting 40
Alamgir 28, 73, 75
Albert Museum 58, 69, 72
album 23, 51, 45, 65, 68, 70, 71, 72, 76
Ali Mardana Khana 68
All'u-l-Katib 36
American collection 69
animal nature 44
animals 22, 31, 32, 42, 45, 46, 52, 53, 55, 56, 57, 58, 59, 65, 66, 68, 69, 70, 76
animals frightened 58
antiquarian 55
Anwar-i-Suhaili 43, 44, 45, 46
applied arts 63
Aqa Reza 44, 51, 52, 57, 81
arabesques 66
Arab horses 69
archaeological excavations 19
architects 40, 55
architectural decorator 65
architecture 20, 22, 41, 55, 59, 63, 65
art 17, 18, 19, 20, 21, 22, 23, 24, 31, 32, 39, 40, 41, 42, 43, 44, 51, 52, 53, 54, 55, 59, 63, 64, 65, 68, 71, 75, 76, 79, 83

art and architecture 41
art and craft 40, 75
art and culture 21, 22, 39, 41, 51
art-historian 17
artist 18, 31, 35, 42, 43, 51, 52, 53, 54, 55, 56, 57, 59, 63, 66, 70, 71, 79
artistic 18, 20, 21, 31, 44, 53, 56, 58, 60, 63
artistically 69
artists 25, 35, 40, 42, 52, 53, 54, 55, 56, 59, 64, 65, 66, 69, 70, 71, 72, 75, 76, 79
art of painting 20, 31, 40, 41, 42, 79
art of peace 40
art of prose 54
arts and industries 40
atelier 51, 56, 58, 63, 65, 71
Aurangzeb 24, 25, 75
Aurengzeb 28, 70, 73, 75, 76, 83
autobiography 32, 52

B

Babar Nama 22, 59
Babur 21, 22, 28, 29, 31, 32, 35, 36, 39, 42, 45, 46, 51, 52, 53, 59, 69
Balchand 52, 68, 81, 82
Basawan 43, 44, 57, 58, 59, 79, 81
beak 71
bear 46, 53, 55, 58, 72
beautiful princes 72
Bedsa 19
bent legs 72
Bhim Gujrati 43
Bhola 68, 82
Bichitr 52, 68, 69, 76, 81, 82, 83
Bihzad 42, 44, 79
Bilal Habshi 43
biographical and religious 44
biographical works 43, 45
birds and animals 52, 53, 55, 56, 58, 59, 65
birds studies 58, 71, 72
Bisandas 44, 52, 56, 81
Bishandas 57
black buck 58, 70
Bombay 52, 57, 70, 72
book-binders 41, 43
borders 51, 65, 68
border style 67
brain child of Humayun 42
branches 57, 58, 59, 70, 71
British Museum 57
broad borders 65
Buddhism 19
Buddhist 19, 20
Buddhist Mahaviharas 20
builder 41, 55, 64
bullock cart 70

C

calligraphed 44
calligrapher 35, 41, 51, 53, 55
calligraphic 51, 65, 67, 72
calligraphist 51
caparisoned horses 68
carpet weaving 63
cave paintings 19
celebrated painter 58
Central Asian 21
Central India 45
chatter of birds 58
cheetah 58
Chela 43, 46, 59, 79, 80, 81

Chester Beatty Library, Dublin 76, 83
Chinar tree 57, 58
Chitraman 68, 82
civilization 20
classical 19, 20, 43
classicism 20
closeness to nature 44
colour 41, 53, 57, 58, 65, 68
coloured folios 51
colour grinders 41
colouring 42
colourist 43
colours tend 66
commanding 76
communication 46
connoisseur 51, 53, 55
connoisseur's eye 53
costliest thrones 63
costume 17, 44
court historians 23
court life 66
court of Shahjahan 66, 68
court painters 54, 63
courts functions 64
craft 40, 44, 54, 75
crafts and arts 63
craftsmen 40, 54, 55
critical mind 53
cultural stagnation 75
culture 20

D

Dara Shikoh 23, 68, 69, 70, 71, 72, 82
Dara Shikoh album 72
Darbar scene 68
dark skinned horses 47
Daulat 44, 52, 53, 56, 57, 79, 81
dazzling jewels 67
Deccan 24
deceased artists 54
decorations 52, 65
decorative arts 23, 63, 64
deer 32
Delhi 20, 35, 53, 57, 75, 76
Delhi court 76
Delhi Sultan 20
delicate drawings 51
Dervish 23
Diwan-i-Khas 65
drakes 72
drawings 51, 52, 68, 70
ducks 32, 71

E

elephants 32, 45, 56, 68, 69, 70
Ellora 19
embellished old structures 63
embellishment in Mughal miniatures 65
embroidered stuffs 63
Emperor 21, 23, 24, 25, 35, 36, 39, 40, 41, 42, 51, 55, 58, 63, 68, 69, 76
Emperor Akbar 39, 40, 42, 51
Emperor Aurangzeb 25
Emperor Humayun 35
emperors 21, 31, 55, 64
emperor Shahjahan 71
engravers 55
epicurean 51
Europe 21
European engravings 65
explorations 19
eye 42, 51, 53, 54, 55, 69
eyebrow 54

F

Farrukh Beg 44, 56, 57, 79, 81
Farrukh Chela 46, 79
Fatehpur Sikri 40
fauna of India 32
fine arts 51, 63
fine drawings of flowering plants 68
finishing 42, 44
Flora and fauna 44
floral designs 65
floral scrolls 65, 66
flora or fauna 64
floricans 32
flowering plants 66, 67, 68, 72
flowers 31, 36, 53, 57, 66, 69, 70, 72
folios 51, 53, 67, 68, 72

G

galloping horses 69
garden plants of India 22, 52
gazetteer of India 22
genre scene 65
geometrical 68
gilders 41, 43
Giver of life 41
gloved hand 68
God's 20
gold beaters 41
golden bells 69
golden lion 69
Govardhan son of Bhavanidas 44
governing 76
Great Grand Mughal of India 64
Great Mughal 27, 28, 31, 36, 77
grey horses 47
Gupta period 19
Gupta-Vakataka 19

H

Hamzanama 42
Hamza-Nama 42
Harati painter 51
Hashim 57, 68, 81, 82
Hashiya decoration 65
Hasim 52
hawk 72, 76
head artist 55, 66
herons 32
highly trained artists 66
Hijri Calendar 67
Himalyan Cheer Pheasant 72
Hindu 20, 21, 40, 45, 46
Hindu and Muslims 40
Hindu Sisodiya 20
Hindustan 39
Hindustani culture 39
Hindustani races 39
historical and biographical 43
hoopoes 32
Horse and groom 46
horses 46, 47, 68, 69
human figures 66, 67
Humayun 21, 22, 28, 33, 35, 36, 39, 40, 42, 43, 51, 53, 79
hunting styles 44, 70, 76, 83
Hussain Naqqash 58

I

illuminators 41, 43
illustrated 20, 22, 23, 42, 43, 46, 53, 59
illustrated manuscripts 20
illustrations 43, 46, 59, 67
immortal in the world 63
imperial painting 64
Imperial patronage of art 75
Inayet 57, 59, 70, 71, 81

India 17, 18, 19, 20, 21, 22, 23, 24, 31, 32, 35, 39, 40, 42, 44, 45, 46, 51, 52, 55, 64, 71, 72, 79
Indian 17, 18, 19, 20, 21, 22, 31, 32, 36, 39, 40, 45, 57, 65, 71
Indian art 18, 21
Indian cultural 18
Indian culture 18
Indian history 31, 32, 36
Indian in spirit 40
Indianised Persian types 69
Indian monarchs 39
Indian people 17, 18, 39
India Office Library 23, 71, 72
Indo-Islamic 22
Indus Valley Civilization 17
Iran 35
Iyar-e-Danish 46
Iyar-i-Danish 42, 44

J

Jahangir 21, 22, 23, 28, 49, 51, 52, 53, 54, 55, 56, 57, 58, 59, 60, 63, 64, 65, 66, 67, 68, 76, 83
Jaina Bhandaras 20
Jain paintings 20
Jalal-ud-din Muhammed Akbar 39
jewellery 63, 65
joys of the senses 64
jungle-cock 72

K

Kabul 35, 51
Kallan (Senior) 43
Kanha 59, 80
Kanhari 19
Kashmir 22
Kesav Gujrati 43
Khandan-i-Timuriya 42
Khass 45
Khurd 43, 79, 80
Khwaja Abdus Samad 79
kingliness 64

L

Lahore 46, 58, 70
Lahori 43, 67
Laila-Majnun 43
Laila-wa-Majnun 44
Lal 44, 68, 80, 82
Lalchand 68
Lallu Lahori 43
landscape 67
large eyes 71
latter Mughal rulers 24
leafless branches 70
leaves of trees 71
life 17, 18, 20, 31, 32, 41, 42, 43, 44, 45, 54, 55, 58, 60, 64, 66, 71, 72, 75
limbs 41, 68
lioness snarls 70
literature and music 35
living art 24, 75
love of art 44
love of nature 44, 45, 53, 64
lover of the beauties 52
lunar years 67

M

magic of Mansur's 71
magnificent beast 69
Mando Firangi 43

Manohar 44, 56, 57, 68, 80, 81, 82
Manohar son of Basawan 44
Mansur 52, 53, 56, 57, 58, 59, 71, 72, 80, 81
manuscripts 19, 20, 23, 44, 45, 46, 59
margin-cutters 41
margin makers 43
margins 52, 66, 67
master 42, 43, 44, 54, 57, 58, 59, 76, 83
Master like Daswant 43
masters 56
mastery of the craft 44
mausoleum 63
medieval period 21
medieval phase 19
medieval phases 20
medieval style 20
metalware 63
Mewar 20
miniature 20, 40, 55, 57, 58, 63, 66, 70, 72, 75
Miniature painting 40
miniature paintings 20
miniatures 21, 23, 44, 51, 52, 57, 65, 71, 76
Mirdost 68
Mir Sayyid Ali 35, 40, 79
Miskin 44, 46, 59, 79, 80
mobile gardens 36
monals 32
monkey 32, 58
monuments 19, 64
mood and behaviour 44
mouse 32
Mughal 17, 20, 21, 22, 23, 24, 25, 27, 28, 31, 32, 36, 40, 42, 44, 46, 47, 51, 53, 54, 57, 59, 60, 63, 64, 65, 66, 71, 75, 76, 79, 83
Mughal atelier 71
Mughal capital 25
Mughal court 51, 59, 75, 79
Mughal dynasty 21, 22, 31
Mughal Empire 24, 75, 76
Mughal era 20
Mughal miniatures 21
Mughal power 22
Mughals 21, 24, 36, 44, 46, 64, 77
Mughal school 21
Mughal school of miniature painting 40
Mughal school of.painting 21, 24, 53
Mughal throne 63
Muhammad Amir Qaziwine 67
Muhammad Faquirullah Khan 66
Muhammad Khan 72, 82
Muhammud Sharif 44
Mullahs 23
Murad 57, 59, 68, 81, 82
Muraqqas 66
musicians 68
music of the birds 53
Muslim religious idioms 41
Muslim ruler 20
mythical stories 42

N

Nadira Banu 44
Nadir-al-Asra 57
Nadir-uz-Zaman 57
Nafahat-al-Une 57
Nal-Damayanti 43
Nand Gwaliari 43, 80
Nanha 44, 57, 59, 80, 81

narrative scenes 43
natural history 17, 22, 32, 57, 58, 71, 72
natural history scientist 22
natural history scientist of India 32
naturalist 51
nature 21, 22, 31, 32, 44, 45, 46, 51, 52, 53, 55, 56, 59, 60, 64
need of art 42
nephew of Nanha 44
new style of painting 40
Night Heron 71
nilgai (blue-bull) 32

O

observer of nature 55
ornamental textile 69
ornithologists 57

P

Padarath 57, 59, 81
Padashah Nama 23
Padshah Nama 67
painted 23, 42, 43, 46, 53, 54, 56, 57, 58, 59, 67, 68, 69, 76, 83
painter 24, 35, 41, 46, 51, 52, 57, 58, 68, 71, 72, 82
painters 21, 23, 40, 41, 42, 43, 44, 46, 52, 54, 55, 56, 57, 58, 59, 63, 66, 68, 71
painting 19, 20, 21, 22, 23, 24, 25, 31, 32, 35, 40, 41, 42, 43, 44, 46, 51, 52, 53, 54, 55, 57, 58, 59, 60, 63, 64, 65, 66, 67, 68, 69, 70, 72, 75, 76, 79
paintings 19, 20, 21, 23, 42, 46, 51, 53, 63, 65, 66, 67, 72, 75, 76
pair of ducks 71
Pala 19, 20
Pala period 20
Panchatantra 46
paper makers, 41
parrots 32
passionate nature 64
patron 23, 41, 63, 68
Payag 68, 82
peacocks 32
pearl tassels 69
pelicans 32
pens 51
Persia 22, 35, 59
Persian books 42
Persian classical 43
Persian in technique 40
Persian Master 40
Persian Masters 35
Persian solar 67
Persian style 21, 42
Persion and Indian cultures 22
pheasants 32
pictorial 40, 56
pictorial art of India 40
picturesque 64, 71
pigeons 32, 72
pink elephant 69
Pitalkhora. Cave painting 19
plants and flowers 66
poet 51, 53
poets 40, 52
poison of ignorance 41
polishers 41
political chaos 75
pomp and glitter 66
portrait 23, 43, 56, 57, 68, 69, 76

portraitist 68
portraits 23, 54, 65, 68, 72
portraiture 17, 23, 68
post-classical 20
powerful animals 68
precious album of miniatures 23, 71
precious stones 65
pre-historic rock paintings 19
prince 23, 51, 64, 65, 71, 72
Prince Dara Shikoh 70, 71
princely 51, 59
Prince of Wales Museum 57, 70, 72
princes and courtiers 67
prize falcon 68
process of life 18, 42
prose and poetry 42
provincial Sultans 20

Q

Qaziwine 67

R

Rajm Nama 46
Ramayan 43
Ramayana 46
Razm-Nama 42
reading 76
recognising God 41
recreation 46
regal majesty 70
retracted neck 71
rhinoceros 32
rituals 44
rock-cut 19
rock paintings 19
Royal Library 67
Royal show piece 69
royal workshops 76

S

Safavid Persian 46
sambhar 58
Sanksrit 46
school 21, 24, 25, 35, 36, 40, 53, 54, 60, 75
school of painting 21, 24, 25, 35, 40, 53, 60
seizer of universe 75
Shah Jahan 22, 23, 24, 28, 61, 63, 64, 65, 66, 67, 68, 69, 70, 71, 72, 75, 76, 82, 83
Shahjahan period 67, 70
Shah Suja 70
Sher Shah 35
Siberian crane 57
signatures of artists 52
Sisodiya ruler 20
Sittannavasal, Kanchipuram 19
social historians 43
socio-cultural 18
son of Khwaja ‘Abd-us-Samad 44
source of wisdom 41
South India 24
sphere of art 75
squirrel 32
state of beauty 53
stems and leaves 65
studies of birds and animals 56, 65
studio 23, 35, 51
style of master 43
Sultan Ali 51
Sultanate mannerism 21
Sultans of Delhi 20
Surat Khana 23
Sur Gujrati 43

T

Tabriz 35, 79
Taj 65
Taswir Khana 23, 41, 43
textile 63, 69
the first master of the age 42
think of God 41
Tirumalaipuram 19
trade 46
trained artists 66
traveling 76
Tumurid 21
Tuti-Nama 43
Tuzk Jahangir 22
Tuzuk-i-Baburi 31
Tuzuk-i-Jahangiri 55
Tuzuk of Jahangir 52

U

unusual fruit 52
Ustad 57, 58, 72
Ustad Mansur 57, 58, 72

V

vegetal and floral patterns 52
vegetal designs 68
Victoria and Albert Museum 58, 69, 72

W

Wakait-i-Baburi 31
wall paintings 20
wantage Album 72
water mark 55
web of human existence 18, 42
white marble 23, 63, 64
wild bird-life 71
wild buffalo 32
wood carving 63
work of art 41, 54, 55
workshop 55, 76, 83
works of art 23, 65, 71
world 42, 44, 53, 63, 64
world's art 44
writers 40, 52

Y

young prince 72

Z

Zafar-Nama 42
Zahir-ud-din Muhammed Babar 21
zoological portraitures 70
zoological statistics 32

Description of Plates

Pl. 1: The White Elephant, Early 17th Century A.D., Bharat Kala Bhavan, Varanasi.

There is a splendid Mughal painting in which the central figure is a pinkey white elephant with Mahavat under a canopy. The white elephant is lavishly ornamental and is shown moving its limbs gracefully. It is attended by two smaller grey elephants fidgeting at a respectable distance, a fully caparisoned horse and a camel led by its drivers are shown nearly.

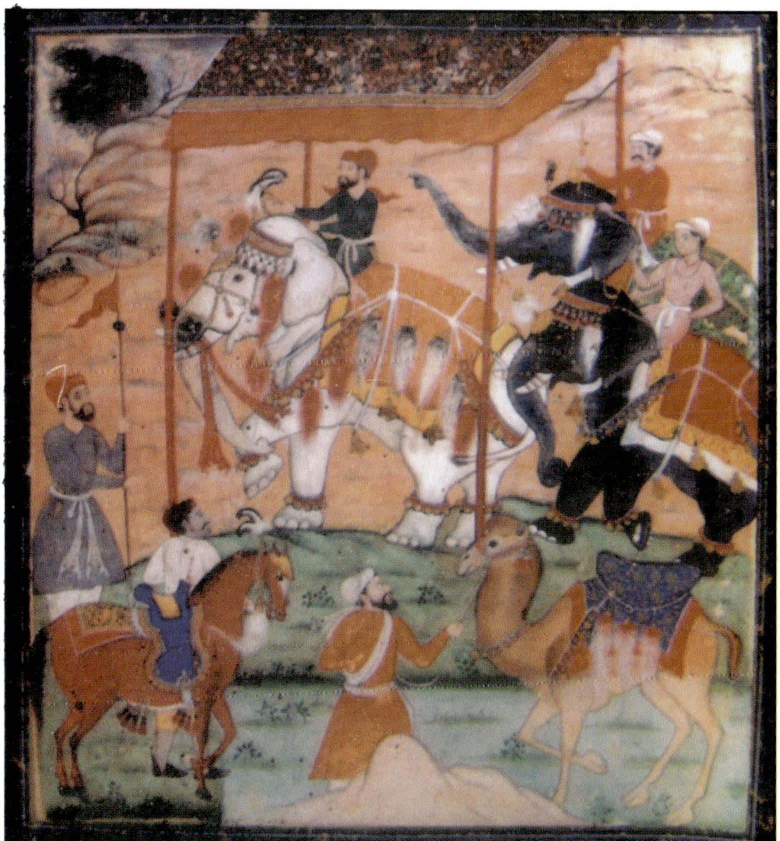

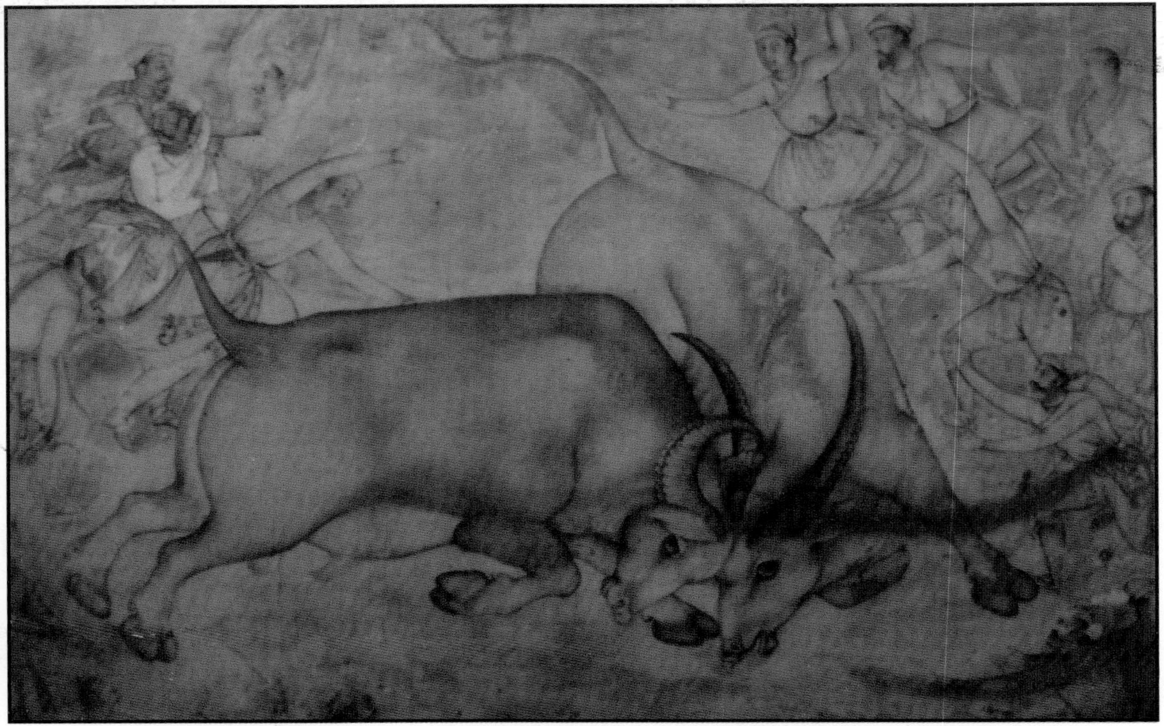

Pl. 2: Bull Fighting, C. 1605 A.D., Artist – Farrukh, Private Collection.

The fighting of bull and deer also fascinated the emperor very much. He, therefore, gave much care to the training of this animal.

In Mughal India, the animal and bird fight had been considered a pleasure sports often ending in a tragedy. Elephant fight is found illustrated in *Babur Nama* and also in *Akbar Nama.* The incidence of elephant fight has been recorded in *Babur Nama.* An illustration shows Babur witnessing elephant fight on the bank of Jamuna. So for Akbar was concerned he watched an elephant fight while on a tour. This event was illustrated by Farrukh with the august portrait done by Basawan. Regarding elephant fight, Manucci made a tacit report in the 3rd quarter of 17th century. He recorded that when king makes them fight (elephants), the wives of Mahavatas remove their ornaments, smash their bracelets and put on mourning just as if they were widows. If their husband come back alive they give a great feast. This refers that on the one hand the elephant fight was taken as a pleasure sport by the king and his nobles, to the families of Mahavats such fight appeared as nightmares terror.

Pl. 3: Elephant Hawaii, C. 1590 A.D., Artist – Composed by Basawan and painted by Chitra.

In a double page composition of a three page of narrative in *Akbar Nama*. Akbar's adventures with the elephant Hawai was composed beautifully by Basawan and was painted by Chitra.

The composition includes the elephants thunder across the bridge of pontoons, the boats capsize with their weight and volume, shouts of alarm pursue Akbar who sits firmly on the said elephant. On the facing page stands Ataga Khan with his silent entreaty and with him a see off hands great and small are raised supplication.

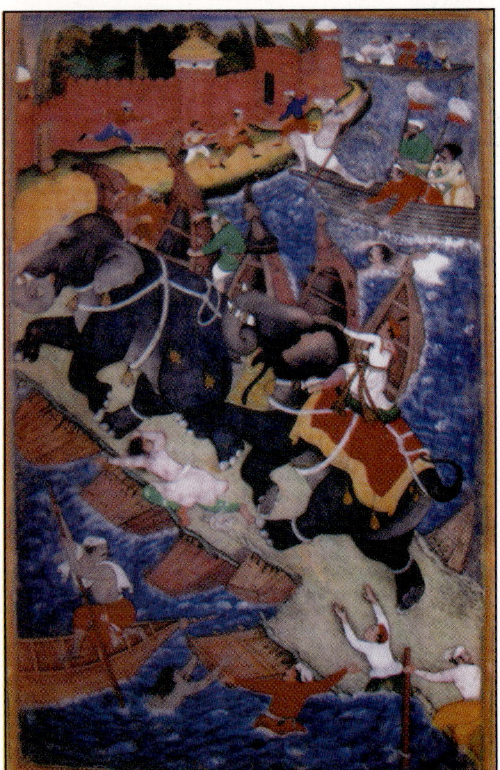

Pl. 4: A Lion Court, Mughal, Artist – Farrukh Chela, Bharat Kala Bhavan, Varanasi.

Painting showing a lion's court. The king lion is seen in the former sitting majestically against the background of trunk of a tree. He is attended by a number of animals shown around him. The animals are shown in pairs. These include pair of lions, stripped tigers, leopards, panthers, hyenas, wild cats, dues and hares etc. A few of these courtiers are attentively listening to the address of king lion while few are seemingly indifferent.

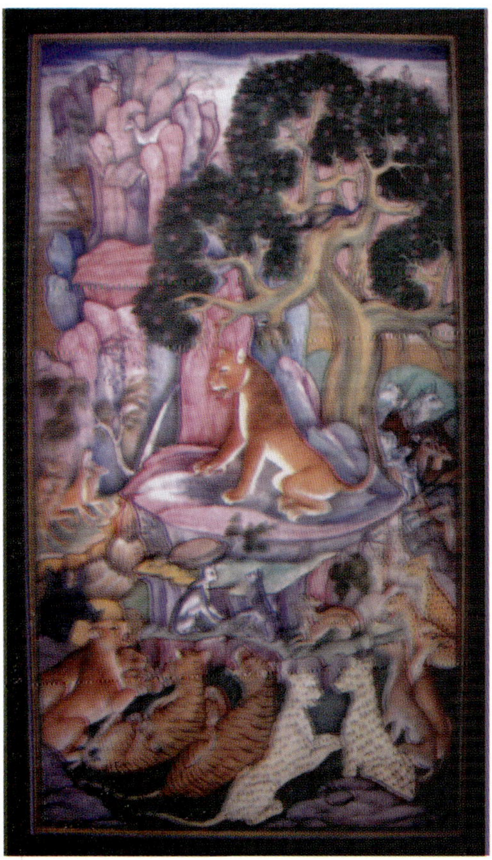

Pl. 5: Lion Court (The Assembly of Animals), C. 1596 A.D., Artist – Miskin, Bharat Kala Bhavan, Varanasi.

In this painting the king lion is given a distinguished seat. The Jackal introduces an ox with the king lion. Some of the courtiers are depicted as attentive, some are indifferent, some are engaged in usual gossips. The animal court here reminds the scenario of contemporary Mughal court and its norms.The roaring lion in all likelihood in this reminds one of emperor Akbar and the ox, likewise stand for a powerful Hindu Raja.

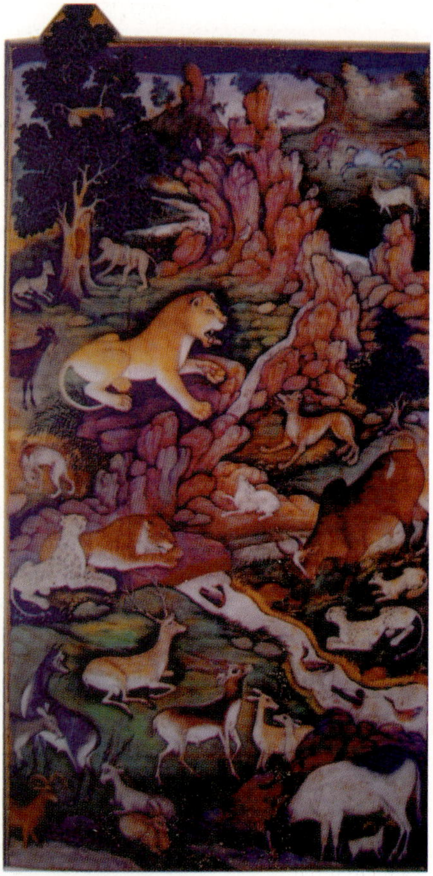

In the painting, an European is shown tending horses on the top left. On the other side at the top a banyan tree predominates alongwith few monkeys. Miskin's animals do not look neither wild and ferocious nor they appear casual or indisciplined. His animals are noticed indifferent poses, postures and actions and these looks very much close to their nature.

Pl. 6: A Carcass of a dead camel, Mughal, Artist – Miskin, Bharat Kala Bhavan, Varanasi.

The painting shows the carcass of a dead camel being consumed by a host of wild carnivorous animals. A few other animals and reptiles are seen watching this gruesome enactment. The story involves a camel who was assured protection by the king lion which it failed to keep. The other jealous animals courtiers worked out a startagem that finally persuaded the king lion to kill the camel.

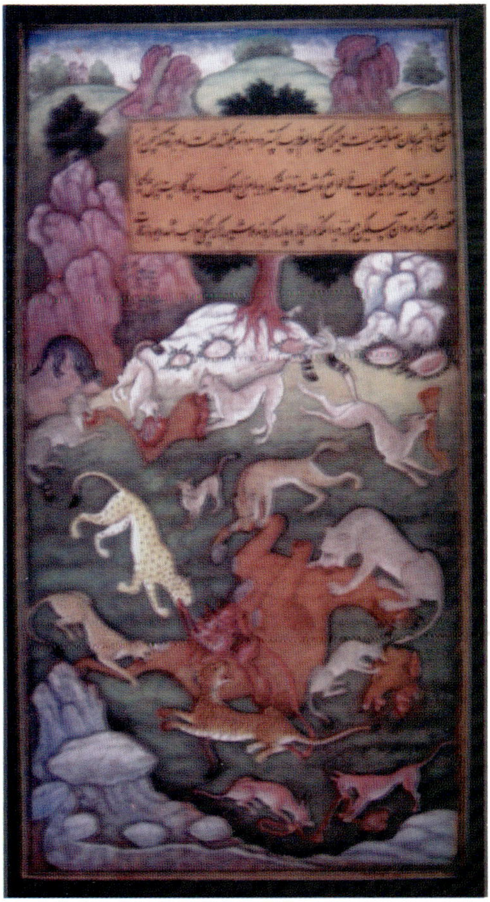

Miskin had attained the height of excellence and therefore, he could portray both dead and live animals, their jealousy, cunningness, their feroceousness, their hunger every thing has been delineated and recorded with evident fidelity. The friendship, the zealousy, the suspicion which are so common in human beings, are also shown present among the animals.

Pl. 7: Killing of helpless bull, C. 1592 A.D., Artist – Nand Gwaliori, Bharat Kala Bhavan, Varanasi.

The human sentiments are shown among the animals in a painting of Nand Gwaliari, where the participants are a lion- the king of animals, the bull, his friend and the jealous advisor of the king lion – a jackal. Jackal created suspicion in the mind of king lion against his friend bull and this ultimately resulted in the killing of helpless bull at the hand of its erstwhile friend lion. When this happened, other animal courtiers remained as silent spectators, grief stricken and unhappy. The artist paid major attention on the two dramatics personals the lion and the helpless bull, the other animals in the scene are summarily treated and they lack natural vervs.

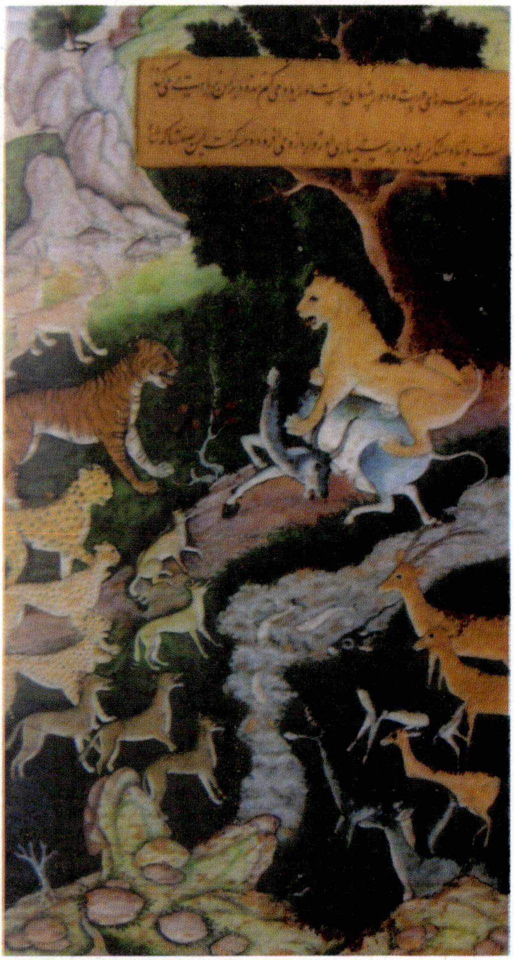

Pl. 8: Camel rider rescuing the Snake, Mughal, Bharat Kala Bhavan, Varanasi.

A painting that shows a kind-hearted camel rider is trying to save a snake from being burnt in a wayside fire. The camel is seen awe strickened by the diagonal movement of fire and the snake is seen equally desperate for its escape from the fire. In the middle part there is village scene where a farmer is seen ploughing with a pair of bullocks, very realistically delineated and the animals are shown completely unaware of the dramatic tension.

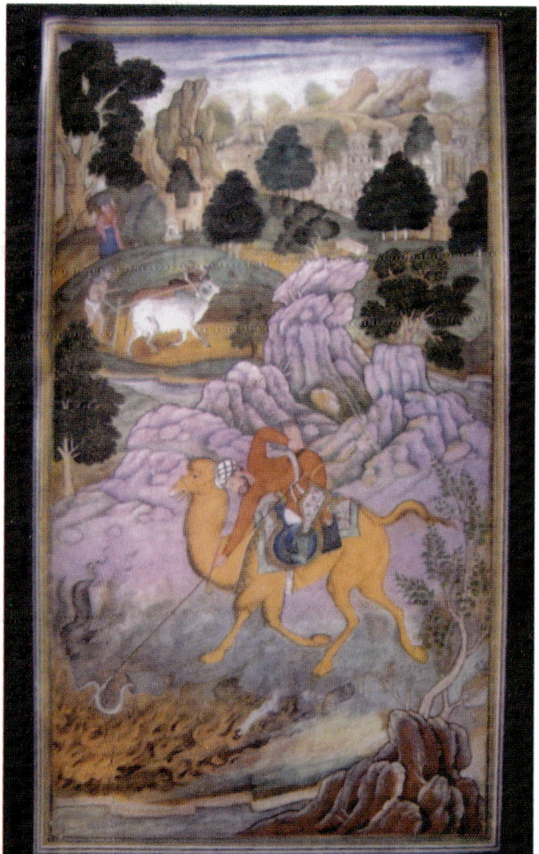

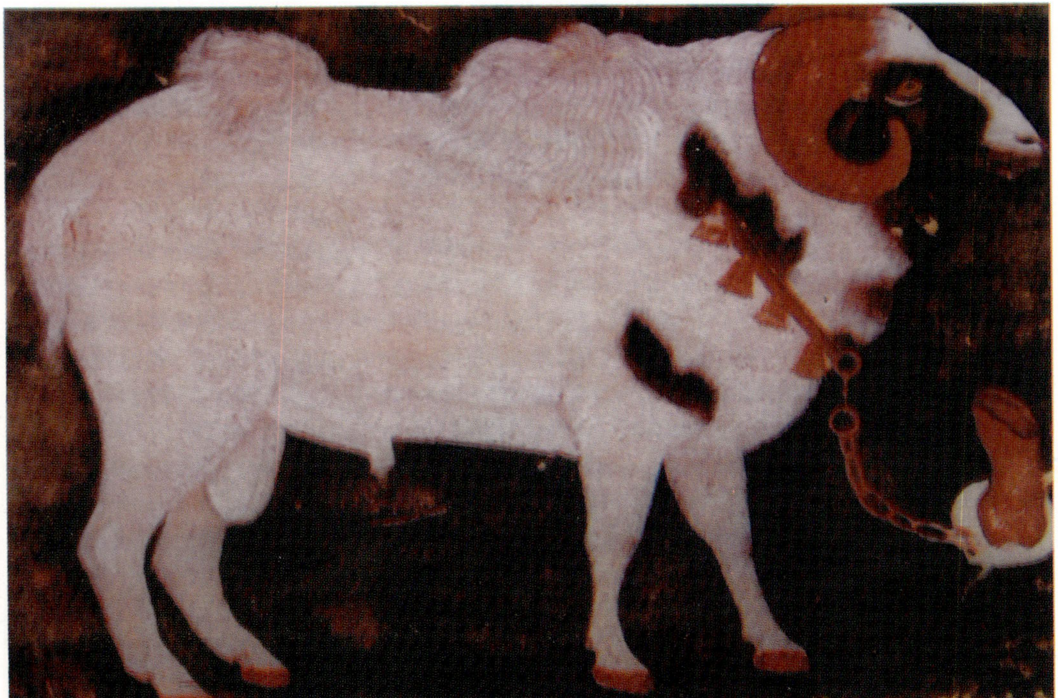

Pl. 9: A Ram, C. 1558 A.D., Artist – Basawan, Maharaja Swai Mansingh II Museum, Jaipur.

Pl. 10: A Story of Old Ass, Artist - Lalchhaman, Bharat Kala Bhavan, Varanasi.

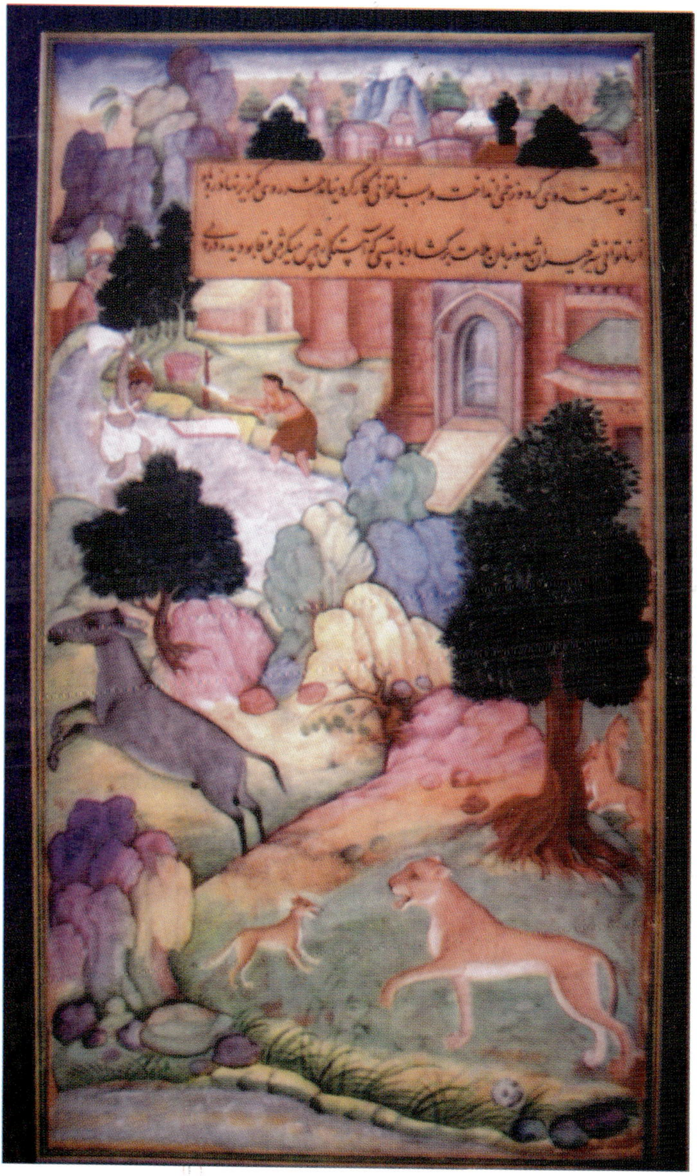

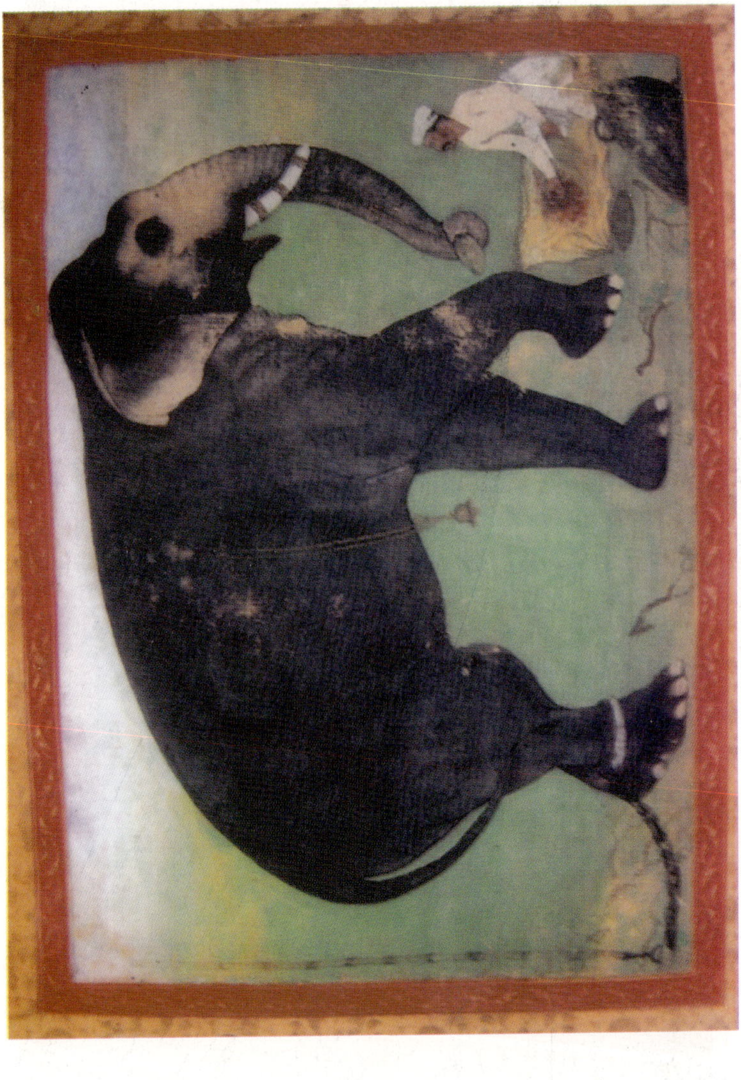

Pl. 11: Elephant, C. 1590 A.D., Artist - Basawan.

Pl. 12: Misconception of Approaching death, Mughal, Artist – Mukund, Bharat Kala Bhavan, Varanasi.

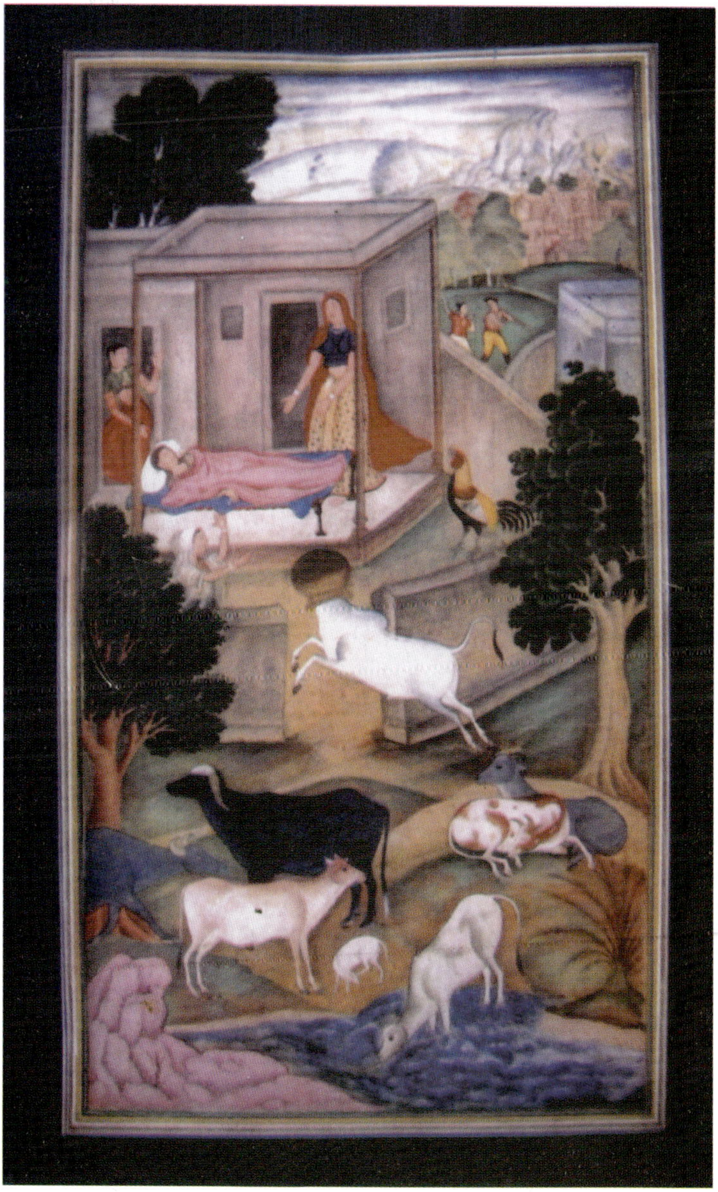

Pl. 13: The farmer retrieves his money miraculously, Mughal, Artist – Bishandas, Bharat Kala Bhavan, Varanasi.

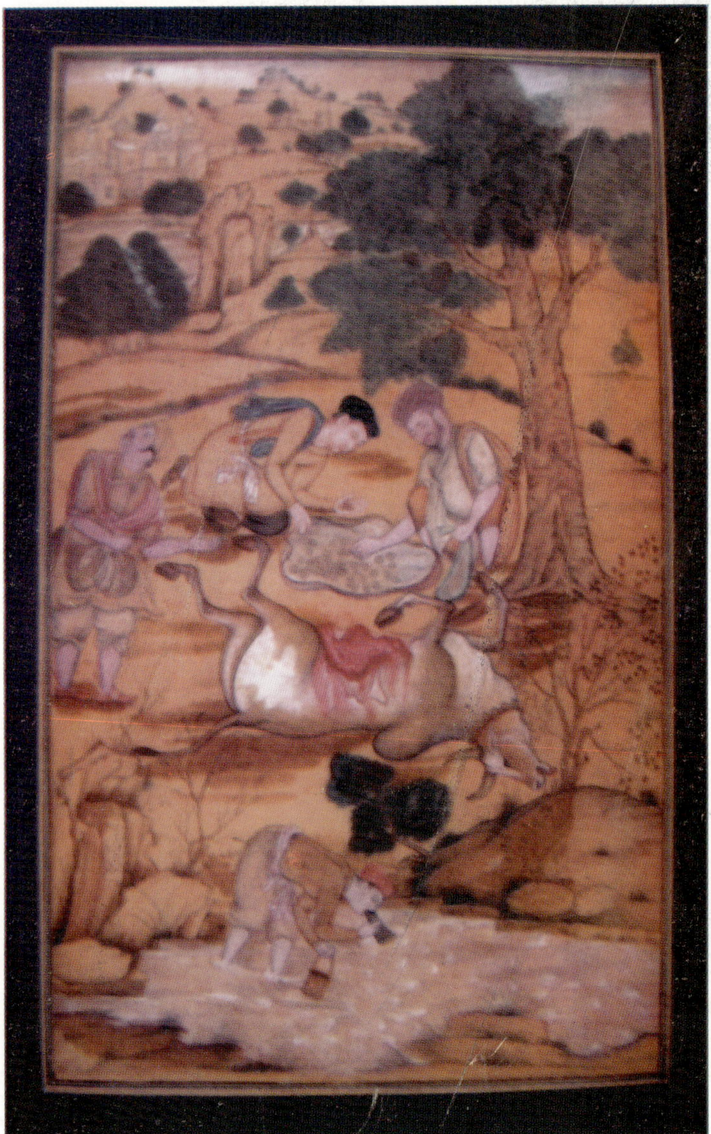

Pl. 14: Mesh Rashi (Aris), Late 16th Cent. A.D. (C. 1570 A.D.), Bharat Kala Bhavan, Varanasi.

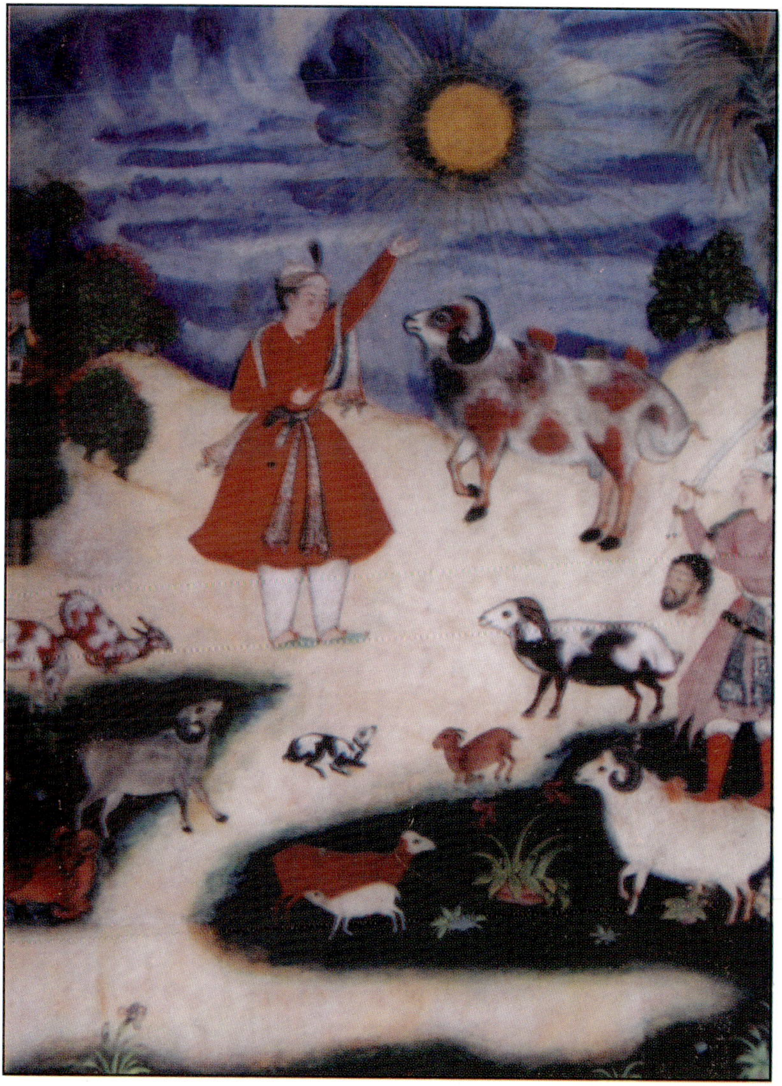

Pl. 15: Jahangir shows his hunting skill, C. 1615 A.D., Artist – Manohar, Indian Museum, Calcutta.

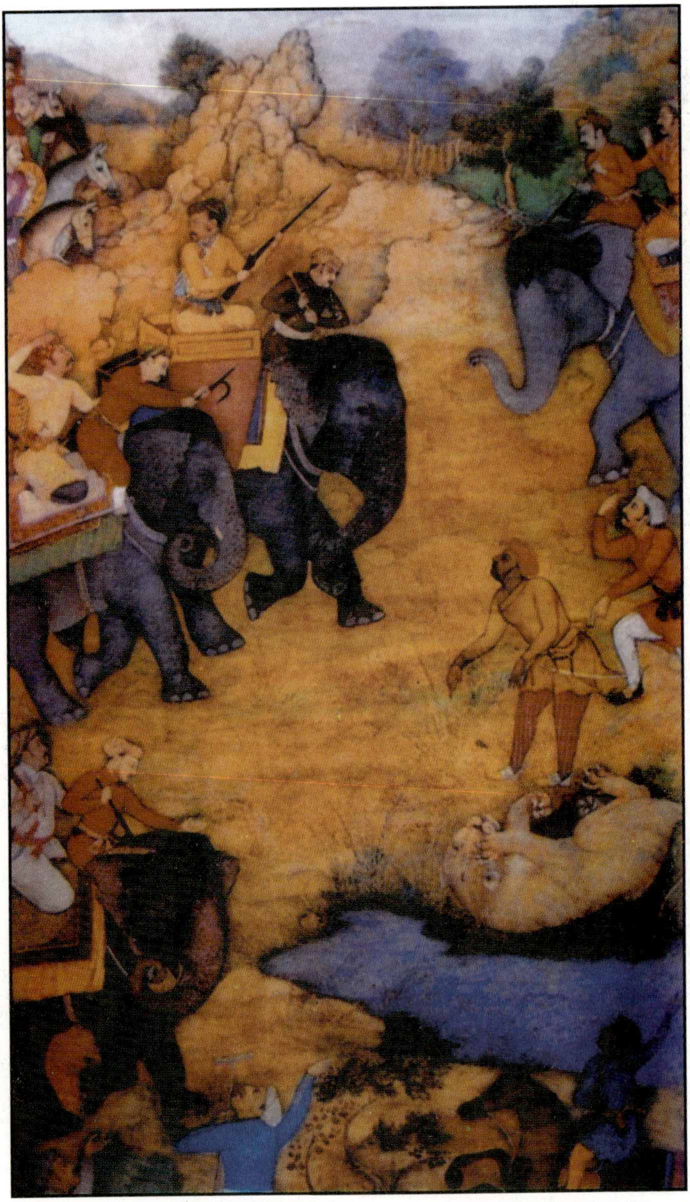

Pl. 16: Emperor on hunt, C. 1598 – 1600 A.D., National Museum, New Delhi.

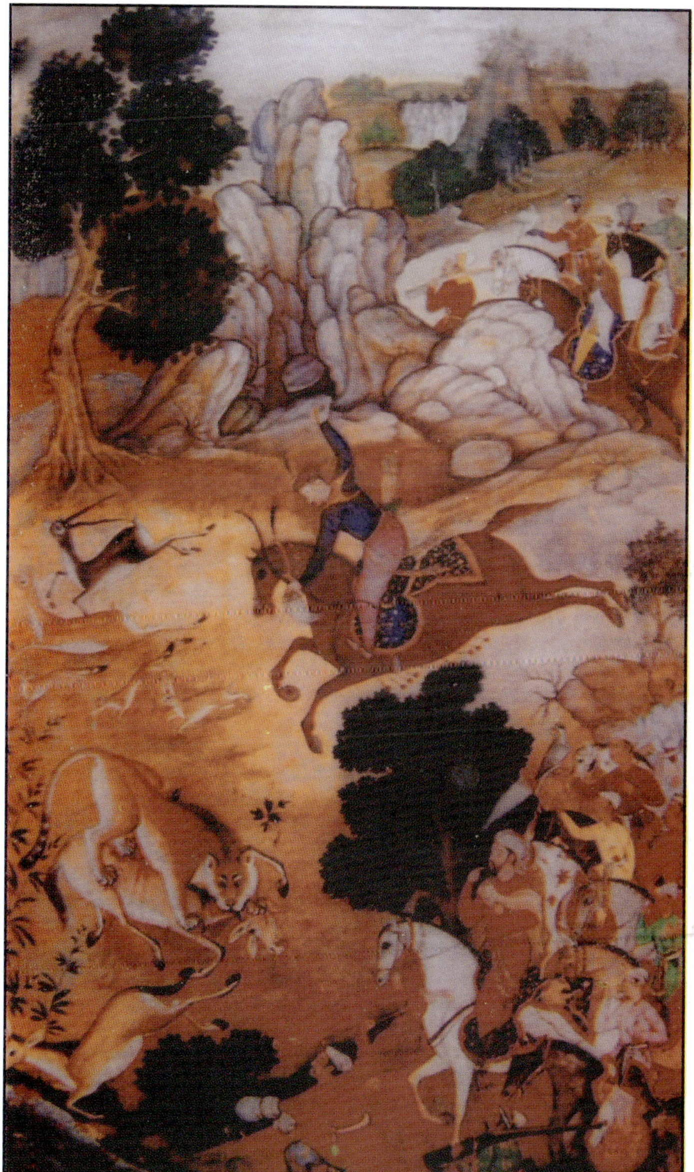

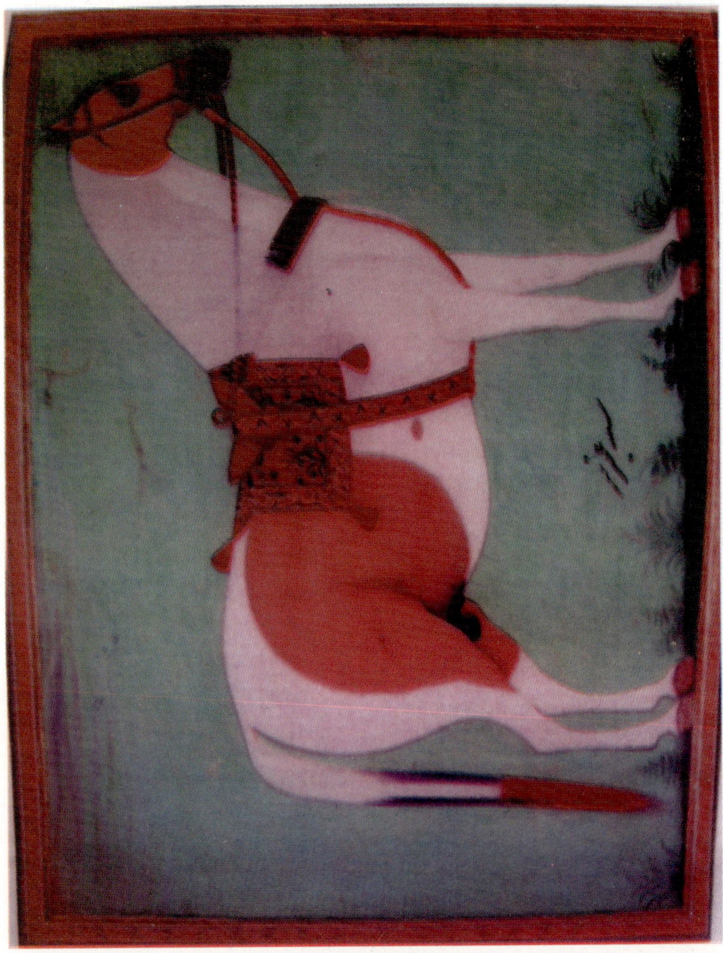

Pl. 17: Horse, Mughal School (Akbari period).

Pl.18: Squirrels in a tree, C. 1615 A.D., Artist - Abu-l-Hasan.

The example shows an extraordinary painting of a Chinar tree with hosts of squirrels in every conceivable position evince the painter's acumen. The artist has painted the spirit as well as the outer form. One can almost here the chatter of birds and animals.

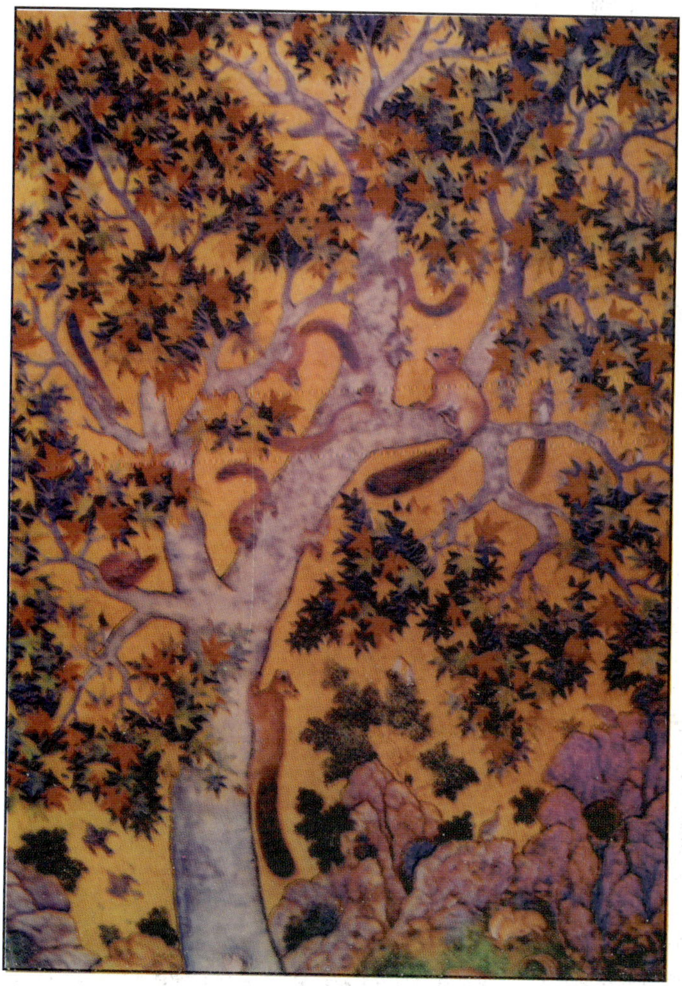

Pl. 19: Falcon, C. 1619 A.D., Artist - Mansur, Maharaja Sawai Mansingh II Museum, Jaipur.

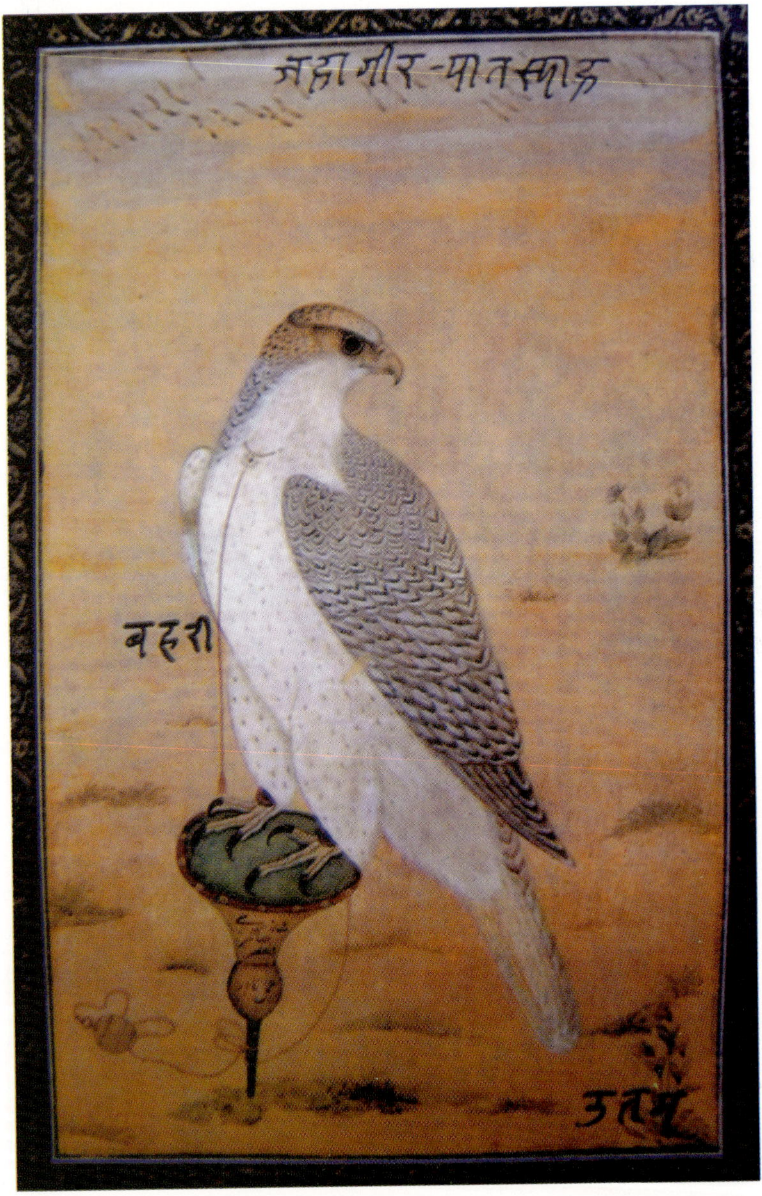

Pl. 20: Falcon (Baaz), Mid 17th Century, Artist - Mansur.

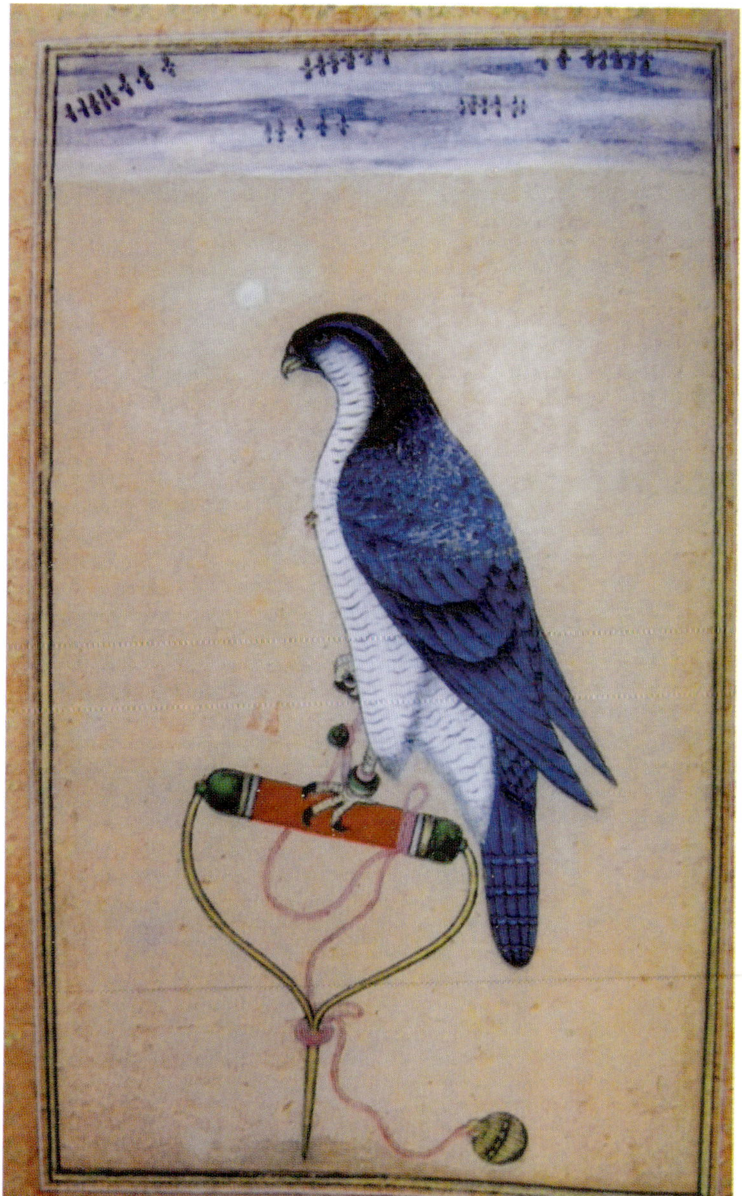

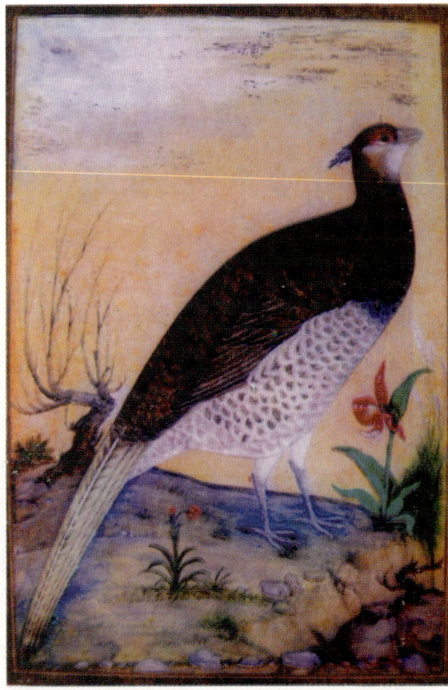

Pl. 21: Himalyan Cheer Pheasent, Circa 1640 A.D., Artist - Mansur, Maharaja Sawai Mansingh II Museum, Jaipur.

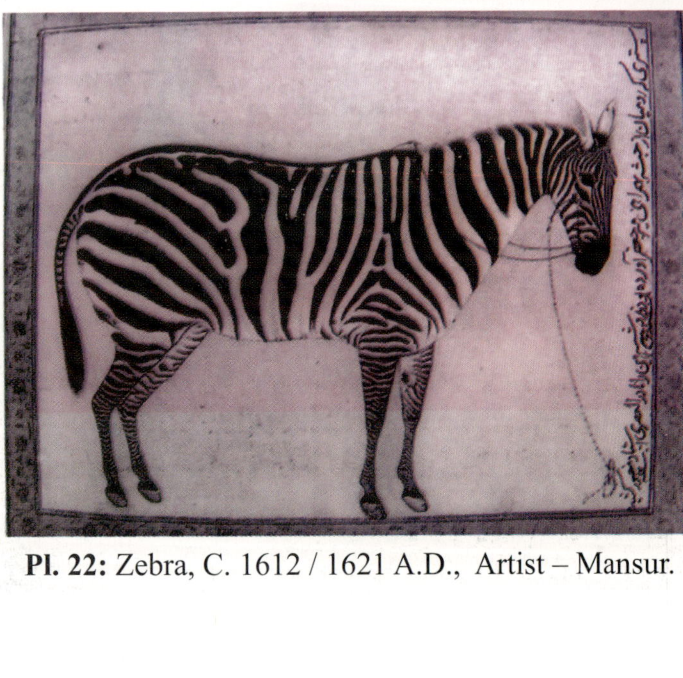

Pl. 22: Zebra, C. 1612 / 1621 A.D., Artist – Mansur.

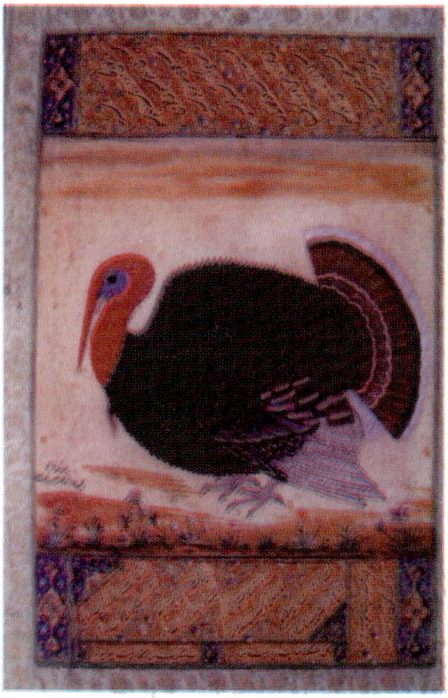

Pl. 23: Turkey cock, C. 1612 A.D., Artist – Mansur, Maharaja Sawai Mansingh II Museum, Jaipur.

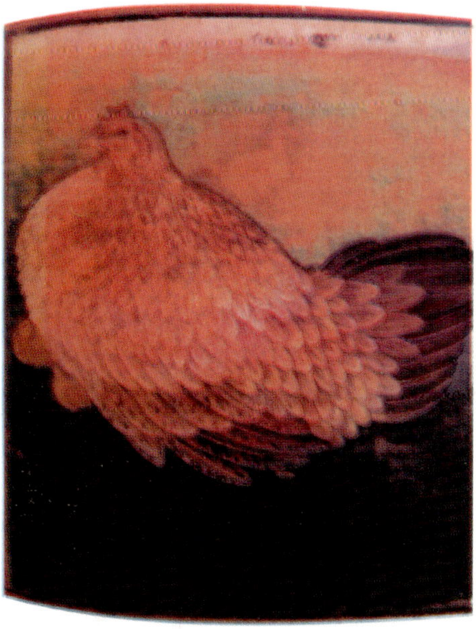

Pl. 24: Hen and Chicks, Mughal School, C. 1605-27 A.D., Artist – Ustad Mansur.

Pl.25: Maina, C. 1625-30 A.D., Probably – Mansur, Prince of Wales Museum, Bombay.

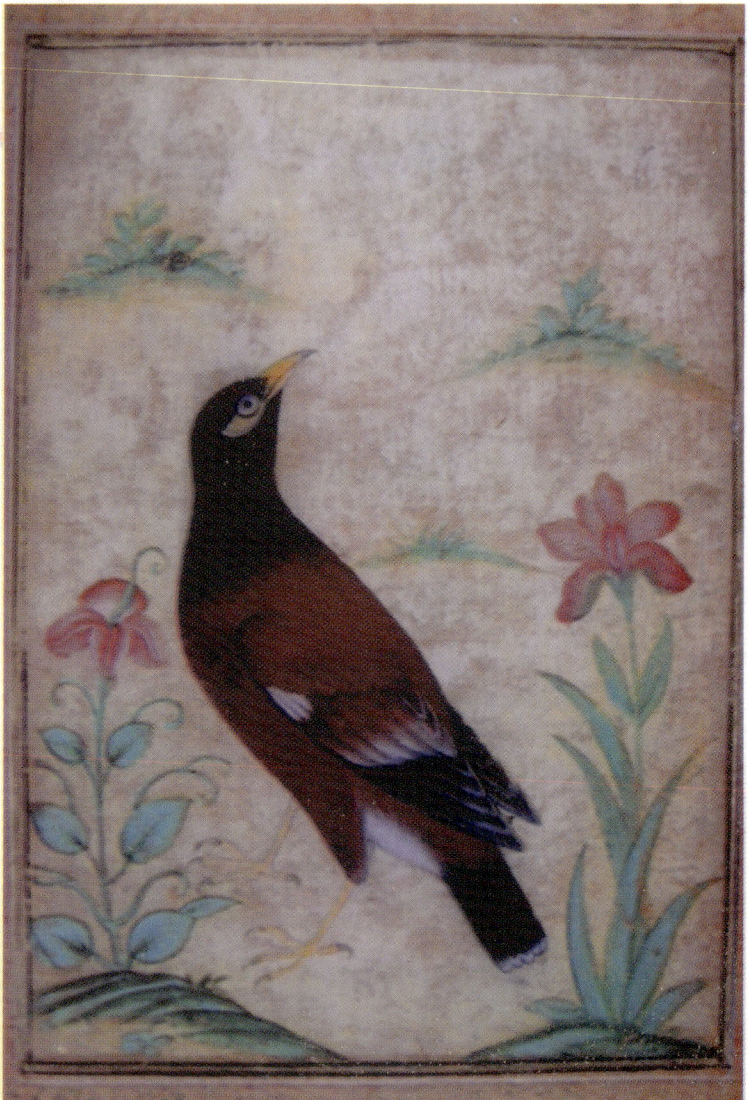

Pl. 26: Jungle Fowl, C. 1611 A.D., Artist – Mansur.

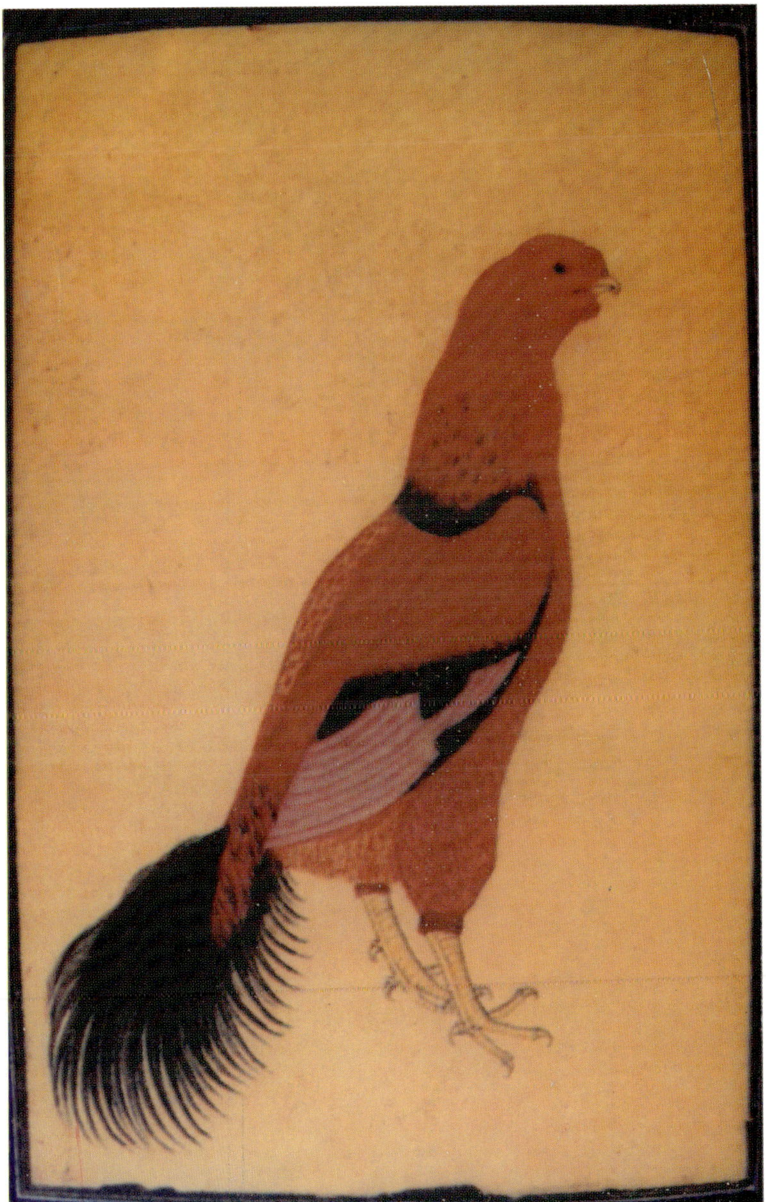

Pl.27: Emperor holding the hawk, C. 1600 A.D., Jahangiri Period.

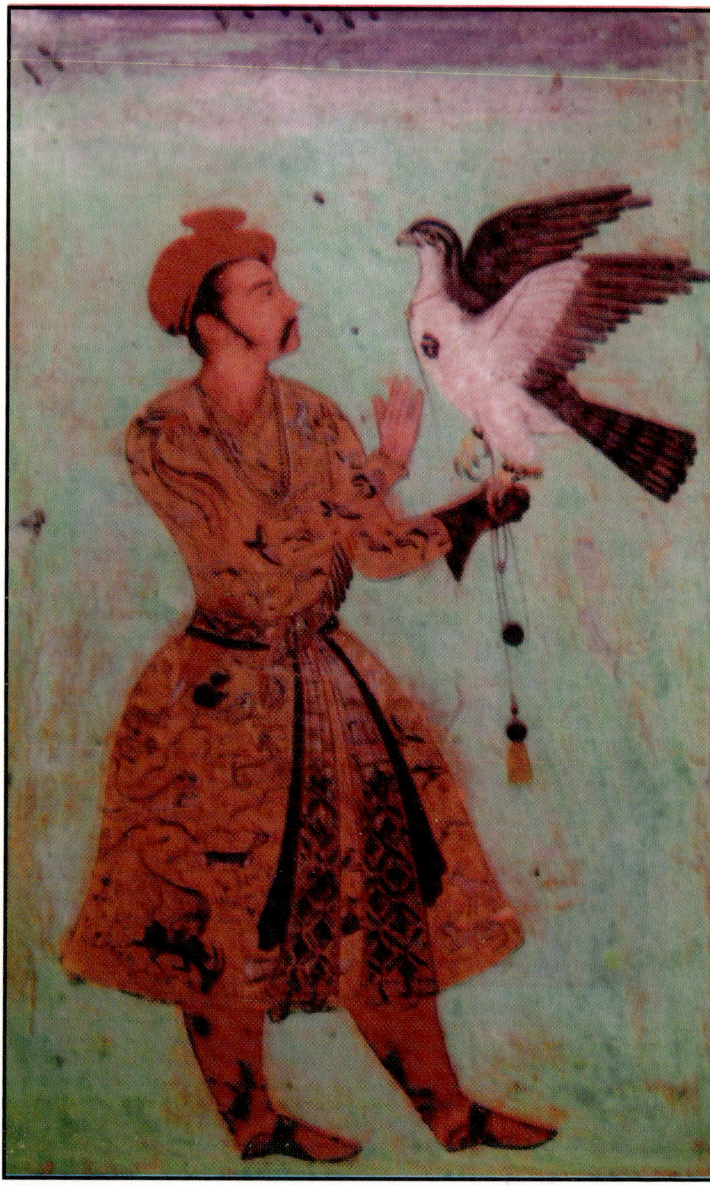

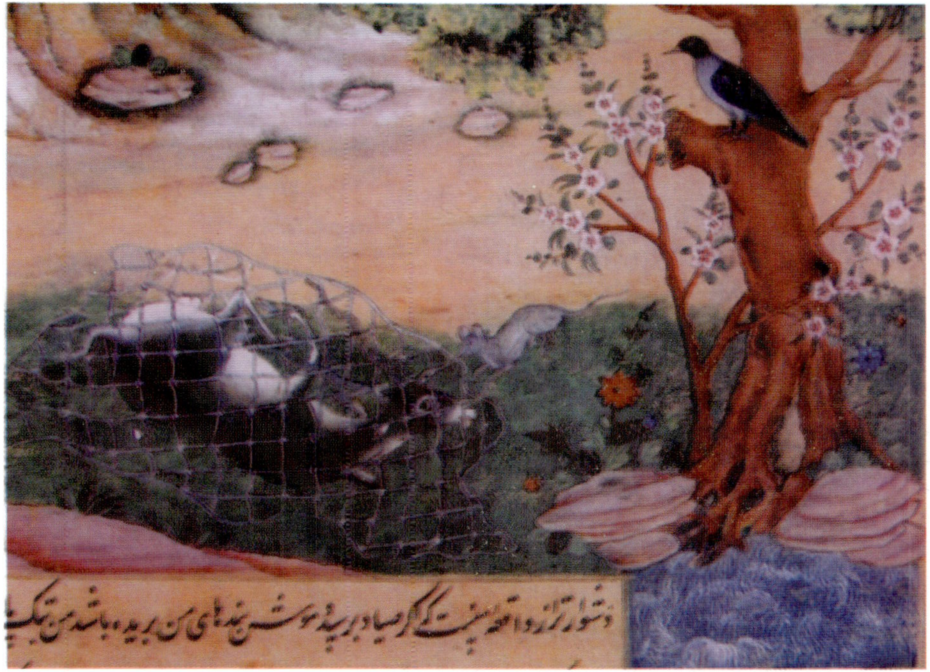

Pl.28: Ensnared Deer, Folio from an illustrated Ms of Anwar-i-Suhali, C. 1575 - 1680 A.D., Prince of Wales Museum, Bombay.

Pl.29: Himalayan Ibex (Mountain goat), Early 17th Cent. A.D., Prince of Wales Museum, Bombay.

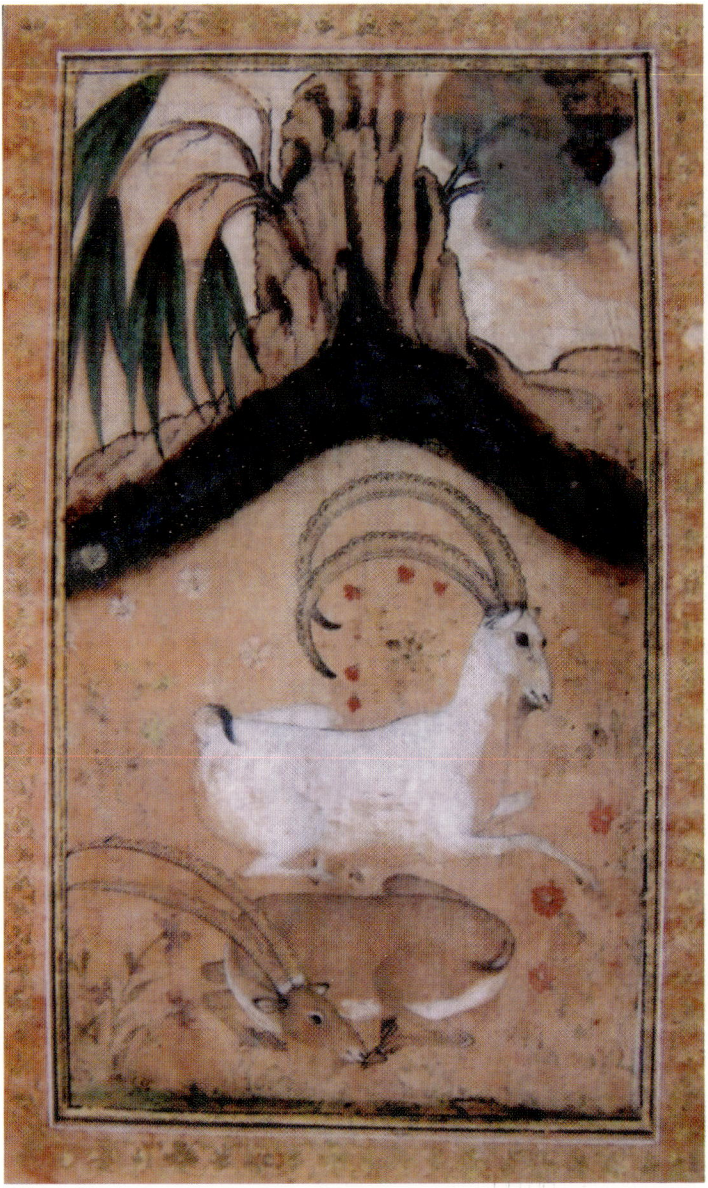

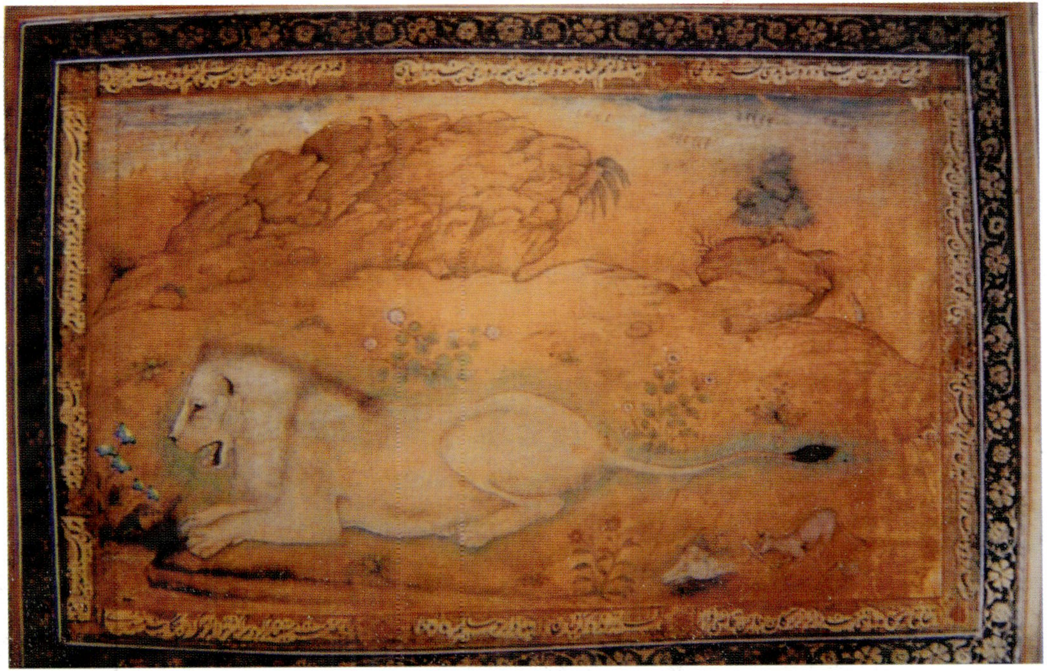

Pl.30: Lion drinking water, C. 1618 A.D., Artist – Nanha, Maharaja Sawai Mansingh II Museum, Jaipur.

Pl.31: Dara Shikoh with Sages, Artist – Bichitra.

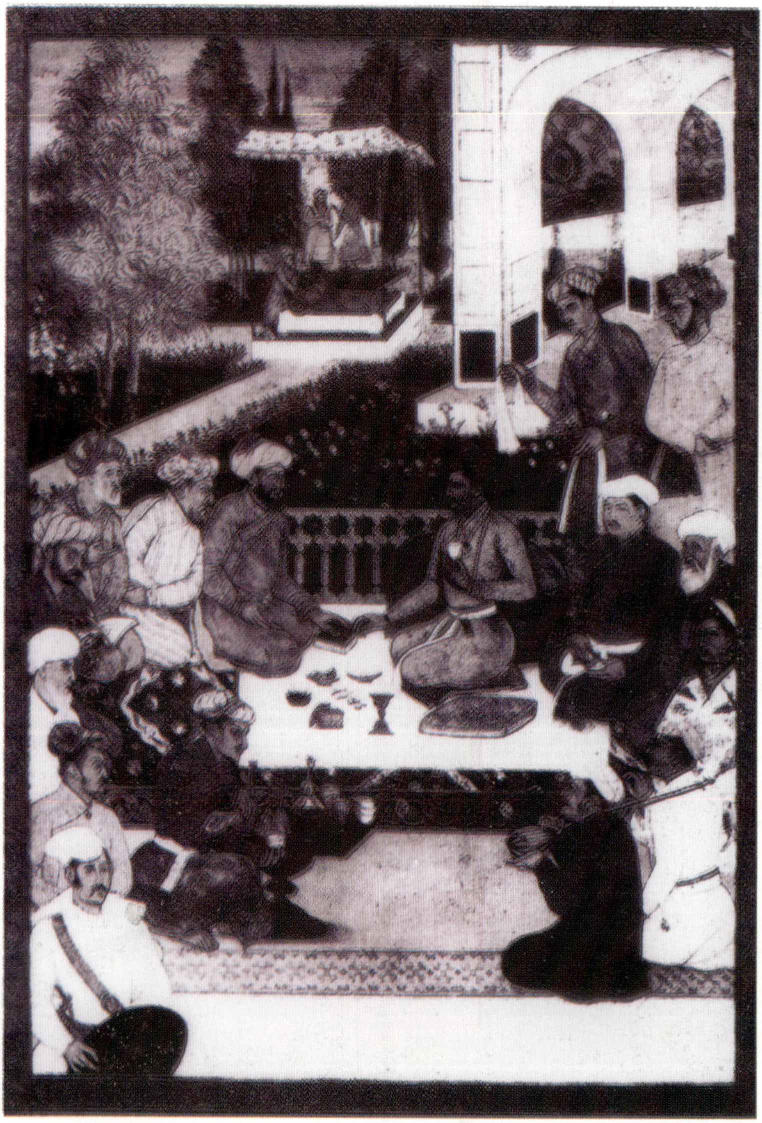

Pl. 32: Darbar of Alamgir (Aurengzeb), Artist – Bichitra, Private Collection.

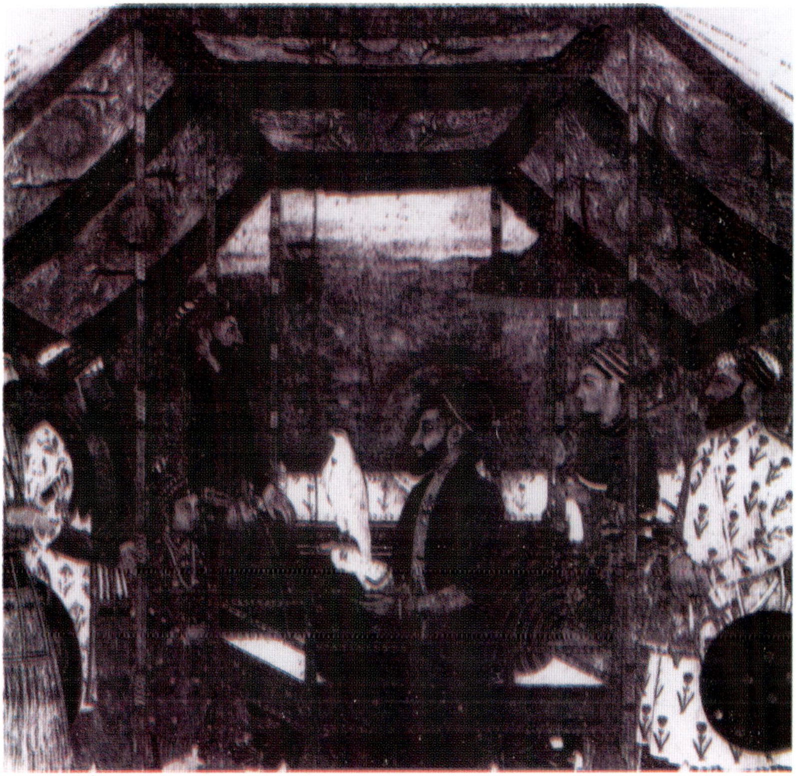

Pl.33 A & B: Aurengzeb Hunting Nilgai, C. 17th Century, Artist – Bichitra, Bharat Kala Bhavan, Varanasi.

The large hunting scene can hardly be bettered in 17th century Mughal art. It was probably painted by Bichitr, the master who had worked for Jahangir and Shah Jahan.

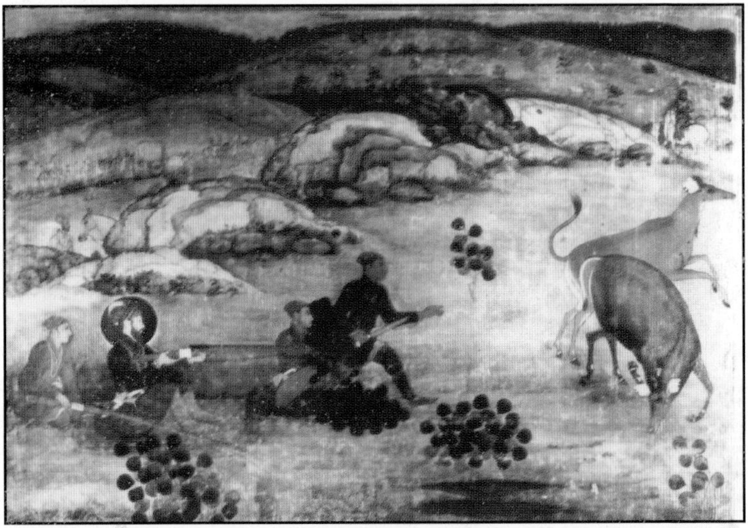

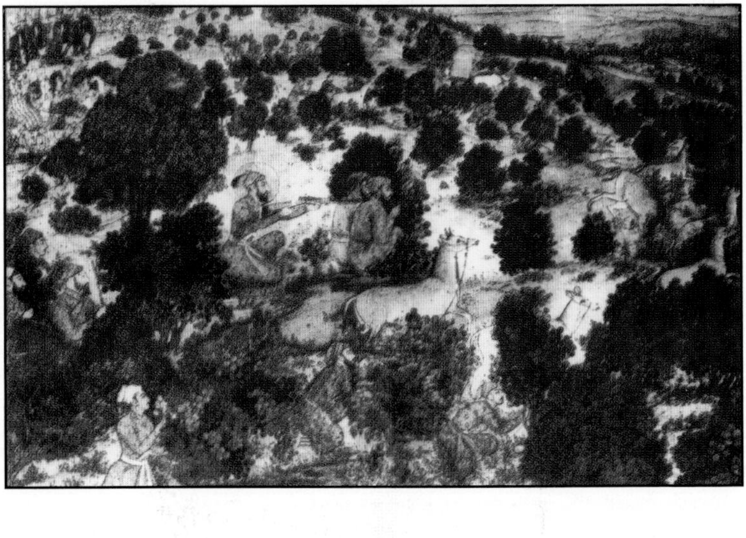